Our Readers Rave

Some books print fancy reviews written by critics. We'd rather share what our faithful fans have to say about UNCLE JOHN'S BATHROOM READERS. Thanks for reading!

"Whenever I say something interesting, my mom will ask if I learned it from Uncle John (or *The Simpsons*)."

—Emily W.

"My aunt made me get a book to read, since I hate reading. And I picked up your book, and now I can't put it down."

—Falon K.

"Thanks for everything. I've been a loyal reader for nine years, ever since Mom brought me the *Legendary Lost Bathroom Reader*."

—Shane G.

"My fifth-grade students want to start a local club!!! They love all the information and facts you give them!"

—Kristie H.

"I started reading *For Girls Only*, and it's really good. I'm a visual person, so I really like the illustrations!"

—Tawny M.

"My friend in school was reading Bathroom Readers, so then I bought a couple. Now my mom says I'm threatening her with my intelligence."
—Chase O.

"I love your For Kids Only book *Did You Know...?* My stepson and I love to read it. It has helped bring up his grades. Keep up the good work."
—Apryl S.

"I'm a thirteen-year-old boy, and I love your BRI series. My favorite book is *Facts to Annoy Your Teacher.* Can you make another one of those books?"
—Noah T.

"I love your books! I have 11 books and I'm just a kid. I take them to school and everyone loves to read them. One time my friend took one of your books off my desk and just started reading. I said, 'Hey give me my stinking book back!' He said 'Geez I was just reading it.' So please write more books!!!"
—Andrew S.

"I love *Uncle John's Bathroom Reader.* I get the new edition for Christmas every year, but for some strange reason I always have to open it last. Go figure."
—Bill C.

"Hey, I love your books so much that in school I'm doing my speech on the history of Uncle John's Bathroom Reader—how it started and where it is today."
—Michelle M.

by the
Bathroom Readers'
Institute

Bathroom Readers' Press
Ashland, Oregon

UNCLE JOHN'S KID-TOPIA
BATHROOM READER® FOR KIDS ONLY

For information, write:
The Bathroom Readers' Institute
P.O. Box 1117
Ashland, OR 97520
www.bathroomreader.com

Design, illustration, and puzzles:
Patrick Merrell
www.patrickmerrell.com

ISBN-10: 1-59223-827-0 / ISBN-13: 978-1-59223-827-9

Library of Congress Cataloging-in-Publication Data
Uncle John's kid-topia bathroom reader for kids only.
    p. cm.
ISBN 978-1-59223-827-9 (pbk.)
1. Curiosities and wonders—Juvenile literature. I. Bathroom
Readers' Institute (Ashland, Or.)
AG243.U525 2012
031.02—dc23
                            2011044540

Printed in the United States of America

First Printing

17 16 15 14 13 12   6 5 4 3 2 1

Thank You!

The Bathroom Readers' Institute sincerely thanks the people whose advice and assistance made this book possible.

Gordon Javna	Joan M. Kyzer
Kim T. Griswell	Melinda Allman
Patrick Merrell	True Sims
Jay Newman	JoAnn Padgett
Brian Boone	Monica Maestas
Trina Hedgpeth	Mana Manzavi
Amy Miller	Annie Lam
Rich Wallace	Sydney Stanley
Kelly Milner Halls	Lilian Nordland
Carly Schuna	Ginger Winters
Nancy Coffelt	Jennifer Frederick
Mark Haverstock	Erin Corbin
Rebecca Shoniker	R. R. Donnelley
Danielle S. Hammelef	Publishers Group West
Angela Kern	Thomas Crapper

Thanks to all the kids who have written to the BRI. Without you, the For Kids Only series would never have happened. If you'd like to be part of shaping future books, send us your ideas at: BRI, P.O. Box 1117, Ashland, Oregon 97520.

Greetings from Uncle John

Welcome to Kid-topia *where kids rule and adults drool.*

Bathroom readers, this book is like nothing you've ever seen. Open to any page, and you'll find something amazing: brain challenges, jokes, puzzles, mind-boggling facts, crafts, recipes, games, mazes, experiments, true stories . . . and much, much more!

In *Kid-topia*, you'll find funny things like . . .

- Why elephants don't like computers,
- What you get when you cross a cow with a waiter, and
- Which comic book hero said, "I hope you're happy. I now have a singed tush."

You'll learn scientific things, such as . . .

- Which dinosaur was the King of Bad Breath,
- Why woolly mammoths need blow-dryers, and
- How scientists plan to get gas from Uranus.

You'll meet amazing animals like . . .

- The biggest dog in the world,
- A seal that talks . . . with a Boston accent, and
- The incredible zedonkulus!

We'll share the inside scoop on . . .

- Why toddlers all over the world want to bite Hermione Granger's head off,
- What scared Draco Malfoy even more than Voldemort, and
- What color Ron Weasley was after being dropped into an icy lake.

We'll teach you how to . . .

- Give yourself rotting zombie flesh,
- Take photos of ghosts, and
- Protect yourself from brain-eating creatures too tiny to see with the naked eye.

Plus, you'll discover . . .

- Games people play with cow pies,
- How maggoty brownies taste, and
- What they serve at the #2 restaurant in Taiwan.

All of us here at the Bathroom Readers' Institute hope your adventures in *Kid-topia* make you smarter, funnier, and taller, just like us!

And remember, when in Kid-topia . . .

GO WITH THE FLOW!

—Uncle John and the BRI Staff

Table of Contents

Brain Games

Bumps in the Night

Dino Dids and Didn'ts

Giggles & Groaners

Gross Me Out!

Hollyweird

Incredible Creatures

In the Game

Just for Fun

Mad Science

Where'd They Go?

Wordplay

Yum's the Word

The Answers

Woo hoo!
Let's get
started.

Caped Comics

Even superheroes sometimes get a laugh.

Batman: If I had any sense, I would've sent you packing.
Spoiler: If you had any sense, you wouldn't be dressed like that.

Wolverine: Hulk, behind!
Hulk: HULK NOT A BEHIND!

"If I wasn't on fire right now, I would have been impressed by that."
                        —Johnny Storm

"Yes, Mr. Death. I'll play you a game! But not chess! My game is wiffleball!"
                        —The Flaming Carrot

"My tush is now singed. I hope you're both happy. I now have a singed tush."
                        —Spider-Man

"Are you seeing what I'm seeing? Because I'm seeing gorillas riding pterodactyls, with harpoon guns, stealing a boat."
                        —Plastic Man

Flash: Ugh—what's that smell?
Wonder Woman: Don't ask.

"Gangway, people! Critically wounded mutant cheesecake en route!"
                        —Blink

The Human Torch: Can we be evil now?
Mister Fantastic: Maybe after dinner.

"And so, may Evil beware, and may Good dress warmly and eat plenty of fresh vegetables."
                        —The Tick

Fowl Facts

Answer on
page 276

Only TWO statements below are true.
Can you figure out which ones?
Go ahead, don't be chicken!

1. ___ True?
If you stacked up all the
chickens in the world,
one atop the other,
they'd reach to Saturn.

2. ___ True?
The University of
Delaware's mascot is
the Fighting Blue Hen.

3. ___ True?
Wild chickens migrate
by walking south in
V formations.

4. ___ True?
Hens that eat a lot of
grass and leaves will
lay light green eggs.

5. ___ True?
In ancient Rome,
chickens were
symbols of bravery.

Hot Dog!

Fun facts about the dogs we love to bite.

Can't Get Enough. Charlie Kazan really loved hot dogs. How much? He ate one nearly every day from the age of 11 months. Here's the amazing part: Charlie lived to be 90. So he ate about 32,000 hot dogs!

Mr. Potato Head's Pals. In addition to the famous spud, toy maker Hasbro created Frankie Frank and his two favorite condiments, Mr. Mustard Head and Mr. Ketchup Head.

Autograph My Buns! Tony Packo's Café in Toledo, Ohio, has served many celebrities. When actor Burt Reynolds showed up for a meal in 1972, Tony's daughter asked for his autograph. Reynolds signed one of Packo's hot dog buns. That started a tradition. Today, thousands of autographed buns hang on the café's "bun wall of fame." A few famous buns: Mr. T., Jerry Seinfeld, and President George W. Bush.

And the Wiener Is . . . Mustard. It's the number one choice of hot dog eaters—33% like mustard better than other condiments. Number two: ketchup (23%). Chili came in third, followed by relish and onions.

On a Roll. Champion racecar driver Al Unser, Jr. took the Oscar Mayer Wienermobile for a test lap at the Indy 500. He hit a top speed of 110 mph.

Giant George

Meet the biggest dog in the world.

Slurp!

Arizona dog lover Christie Nasser wanted a new puppy, but not just any puppy. She wanted a BIG puppy—a Great Dane. So in 2006, she and her husband, Dave, paid $1,750 for a 7-week-old, 17-pound puppy named George. The feisty pup had blue eyes, gray fur, and enormous paws. He gave wet slobbery licks to show affection. For the Nassers, it was love at first sight.

Big Trouble

Three months later, the honeymoon was over. George was sweet but big, and growing bigger. He howled like a banshee if left alone at night. He knocked things over with his whiplike tail. He skittered across the wooden floors. He drenched the furniture in slobber. And he was already the size of a full-grown Labrador. "Everything about owning a dog had become one big problem," said Dave Nasser.

Dave put an ad in the newspaper to find George a new home. Dozens of people responded. But his wife was heartbroken. And then George stared at him with those big blue eyes as if he knew he was about to be carted away. "I balled up the ad," Dave said, "and launched it into the trash."

Super-size Star

Today, George is fully grown. And he's big. How big? He's 7 feet long from nose to tail, and his shoulders stand almost 4 feet above the ground. He weighs almost 250 pounds. (That's 100 pounds heavier than the average Great Dane.) But Dave didn't realize how big George had grown until he took him to the circus. What he discovered: George was bigger than the lions.

Giant George is listed as the world's tallest dog in *Guinness World Records 2011*. He has 75,000 Facebook fans, 2,500 Twitter followers, and 5,000 visitors a day to his website. Even though he's a star, Giant George can still cause a stink. When he appeared on *The Oprah Winfrey Show*, George gobbled up a plateful of pastries before going on the air. And then, he let out a great big rumbling fart.

Great Facts about Great Danes

• Great Danes aren't from Denmark. They come from Germany, where the breed is called *Deutsche Dogge*.

• They're a mix of Irish wolfhound, greyhound, and English mastiff, and were bred for hunting wild boar.

• President Franklin D. Roosevelt had a Great Dane while living in the White House. Its name: President.

• Two famous cartoon dogs are Great Danes: Marmaduke and Scooby-Doo.

The #2 Restaurant

*The theme may be disgusting,
but the food is yummy.*

Hooray for Bathroom Reading!

One day, while sitting on the toilet reading a manga called *Dr. Slump*, 29-year-old Wang Zi-wei got an idea. In the comic book, a robot character named Jichiwawa loves to play with poop and swirl it on a stick. Wang's idea: Sell chocolate ice cream swirls in containers shaped like toilets.

In 2004, Wang opened Modern Toilet restaurant in Taipei, Taiwan. Diners sit on commodes (with the lids closed). .They eat soups and spicy curries from bowls that look like mini toilets. They drink from containers shaped like urinals. On the dessert menu: "diarrhea with dried droppings" (chocolate shaved ice) and "green dysentery" (kiwi). As for the chocolate ice cream? It's served in a swirl that looks like poop.

What the Customers Say

- "There's poop everywhere! Y-u-c-k."
  —Jordan Lien, age 6

- "It's a little gross when you see other people eat, but when you're eating, you don't notice."
  —Chen Kin-hsiang, teacher

- "I will not eat on the toilet!"
  —an elderly diner

Answers on page 276

Say Uncle

The answers below are spelled using only the letters in UNCLE JOHN'S. Use the clues to figure out each one.

U	N	C	L	E
J	O	H	N	S

4-letter answers:

1. _ _ _ _ : ice-cream holder

2. _ _ _ _ : gas used in glowing signs

3. _ _ _ _ : "That hurts!" sound

4. _ _ _ _ : canyon sound rebound

5. _ _ _ _ : bit of information for a detective

5-letter answers:

6. _ _ _ _ _ : nearby

7. _ _ _ _ _ : meal eaten at school

8. _ _ _ _ _ : what shovels make

9. _ _ _ _ _ : building a family might live in

10. _ _ _ _ _ : 1/16 of a pound (weight)

19

King of Bad Breath

When T. rex opened his mouth, the other dinosaurs fled. But maybe it wasn't his teeth that scared them away.

A Killer Crush

Scientists have long thought that *Tyrannosaurus rex* was the most terrifying predator ever known. Big as a school bus, *T. rex* had a 4-foot-long jaw filled with bone-crushing teeth the size of bananas. With a single bite, it could rip off a 500-pound chunk of flesh. If a tooth broke off, no problem. Another would grow back in its place.

But recent discoveries have caused some scientists to question the "Tyrant King" theory. Maybe *T. rex* didn't chase down and kill its prey. Maybe the gunk between its teeth did the fighting for it.

That Really Bites

Some scientists think *T. rex* might have had "septic bite." When meat got stuck between those big teeth, it would have rotted. (After all, dental floss wouldn't be around for another 85 million years.) The rotten meat would have caused bad breath—and something much worse. When *T. rex* bit another dinosaur, the bacteria between its teeth could have gotten into the wound and caused an infection. Then all the giant carnivore had to do was wait for its dinner to die.

Jack Horner, a dinosaur expert from Montana,

thinks *T. rex* wasn't even a predator. Top predators are rare, Horner says. But *T. rex* fossils are very common in North America. Horner says the big meat-eaters were "a dime a dozen."

There's no clear evidence that tyrannosaurs could even run. Given its size, some think all *T. rex* could manage was a fast lumbering walk, kind of like an elephant. It's hard to catch fleeing prey at that pace.

Smell Ya Later

Dinosaur bones have been found with *T. rex* teeth still stuck in them. Scientists say that proves *T. rex ate* other dinosaurs. But it doesn't prove the giant was a *predator*, an animal that kills and *then* eats its prey. Maybe *T. rex* was a *scavenger*—an animal that eats animals that are already dead.

What could prove that *T. rex* preyed on other dinosaurs? Suppose a fossilized bone was found with *T. rex* tooth marks in it (but the bone had healed). The healed bone would show that *T. rex* had bitten the dinosaur while it was still alive, the dinosaur got away, and its bone healed. So far, no such fossil has been found.

Besides big teeth, *T. rex* also had big *olfactory lobes*—the part of the brain used for smell. And it had legs made for walking long distances. There *is* a modern animal that has a great sense of smell and goes long distances to find food: the vulture. Jack Horner says *T. rex* could have been "a huge skulking scavenger with bad breath."

Answers on
page 276

Drop Down and Give Me Five

To solve these puzzles, drop the letters straight down,
not necessarily in the same order as they're stacked.
If you do it correctly, an animal fact will be spelled out.

Sample:

| S | I | L | E | | | H | N | | K | R | E | S | |
| W | L | E | D | P | C | I | I | | C | T | E | N | E | S |

| W | I | L | D | | C | H | I | C | K | E | N | S | |
| S | L | E | E | P | | I | N | | T | R | E | E | S |

1

| | A | T | Y | | H | A | N | N | | S | | E | A | S | | |
| C | A | N | S | T | C | I | N | G | O | T | W | T | E | T | T | E |

2

| | S | | G | A | O | L | E | | | F | | S | O | U | E | S |
| I | A | | C | R | L | U | P | D | O | A | | F | K | X | L | K |

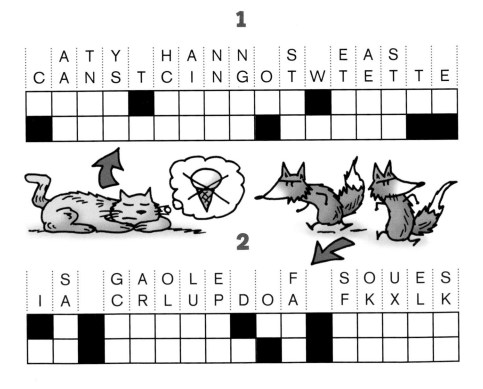

3

C		B		W	D		G	A		O	E			E	O	N
A	A	N	A	L	E	I	E	H	G	L	N	E	N	T	S	T

	■					■						■				
			■						■				■			

4

	E	R	V		B	S		A		D		D	A	T	T	
B	A	A	E	E	R	O	T	H	N	R	O	R	E	N	S	S

							■				■					■
■				■					■							

5

T	I	E	~~Y~~		D			L	E		~~W~~		T	E	R	
~~H~~	H	M	P		S	O		P	N	N	D		L	E	S	N
T	I	P	E	O	O	~~N~~	S	I	A	N	D	A	T	~~H~~	A	S

H						■						■				
				■		N	■					■		H		
			Y	■			■			■	W					■

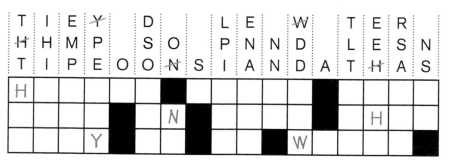

World Wide Weird

Odd facts about people from around the world.

- French people eat about 200 million frogs a year.

- Nine out of 10 British children stay indoors for most of the weekend.

- Every three minutes, someone on Earth reports seeing a UFO.

- One out of every 3,400 Americans is an Elvis impersonator.

- In Tibet, women have long silver pins for picking their noses.

- Canadians eat more donuts than people in any other nation in the world.

- Seventeen percent of Americans admit to peeing in a swimming pool.

- Bulgarians rate the *chushkopek* (an appliance for roasting peppers) the 20th century's best device—over cell phones, TV, and . . . electricity.

- Every four seconds, someone on Earth opens a can of Spam.

- In Afghanistan, more people have cell phones than flush toilets.

- One in three dog owners talk to their pets on the phone.

Woof.

Eat a Banana Slug

How does a slippery, slimy slug feel sliding down your throat? Here's a tasty way to find out!

What You Need:

- Plate
- Spoon
- Butter knife

Ingredients:

- 1/2 cup vanilla yogurt
- Banana
- 2 pretzel sticks

Preparation:

1. Scoop out 1/2 cup of vanilla yogurt onto a plate, and use the back of your spoon to spread it around evenly.

2. Cut your banana in half the long way with a butter knife. Eat one half, or put it in a plastic bag in the fridge to make another slug later.

3. Lay the other banana half in the middle of the vanilla yogurt, cut-side down. Poke two pretzel sticks in its head for antennae.

4. Take a deep breath before you slip the slug onto your tongue!

American Mummies

A tisket a tasket, a coffin or a casket?
OK. That's not how the rhyme goes, but it got
you to look at this slice of coffin history.

A Long Way from the Nile

One day while plowing a field, a farmer in Tennessee dug up something that looked a lot like an Egyptian mummy case. A Georgia man found another case along an eroded river bank. Workers in Virginia found one while installing a gas line. And an Alabama road crew found three more. What were mummies doing in America? Here's what researchers dug up.

Dying to Buy

Before the Civil War, most Southern families buried their loved ones in simple pine coffins made by local undertakers. In 1840, one of those simple coffins would have cost about $2 ($43 today). But by 1850, rich families had a fanicer option.

American inventor Almond D. Fisk created a body-shaped iron casket. The metal was molded to look like the body had a cloth draped over it. The iron caskets weighed 300 pounds. And they cost up to $170 ($4,400 today). The most expensive models had a clear glass window so family members could view their loved one's face.

Afterlife Bonus

Iron caskets had an advantage over pine coffins. Pine boxes let air in, and bodies decomposed. Over time the flesh rotted away leaving only a skeleton. Fisk's caskets were sealed with lead. That made them airtight and kept the bodies "fresh."

Researchers at the Smithsonian recently took a close look at a body buried in an iron casket. When the lid was lifted, the body inside looked a lot like an Egyptian mummy. And it was very well preserved. "Its flesh is still supple, and you can move it," said scientist Dr. Hunt.

5 Creepy (but Real) Coffins

1. The glass coffin. Air-tight glass coffins let people view the body, just like Snow White. (Caution: If you use one, a bunch of dwarves might show up.)

2. The papier-mâché coffin. Cheap, and it's a good way to recycle all those old newspapers.

3. Pre-used coffins. If you don't mind a coffin that's had a body in it, rent a fancy one. After the funeral service, move your loved one to a cheaper coffin.

4. Flesh-eating coffins. The ancient Greeks used limestone coffins so bodies would decompose (rot) faster. Sort of a like a composting coffin.

5. The life-preserving coffin. Some coffins are rigged to pop open if the body inside moves. (Yikes!)

Splat!

This is what the counter looks like after a day of filling orders at the Hot Dog Hut. Can you find a way from the bottle of mustard to the last, unsold frank?

End

Answer
on page 283

Beep! Beep!

Think a bird that runs 18 mph is odd?
You don't know the half of it.

That Bird Is Cuckoo

"Roadrunner" seems like the perfect name for a bird that's so fast it doesn't need to fly. But its official name is *Geococcyx californianus*. Back in the 1800s, this long-legged member of the cuckoo family would race covered wagons—the same way dogs chase cars now. Settlers headed to California gave the wagon-chasing bird its common name: roadrunner. At top speed, the roadrunner takes 12 steps per second. Its feet look like they barely touch the ground.

Table Manners? Not!

Roadrunners have another name: "snake killers." That's because they're fast enough to catch snakes— even rattlesnakes—and they love to eat them. How does a roadrunner kill a rattler? It grabs the snake by the tail, cracks it like a whip, and slams its head against the ground until it dies.

The bird eats its prey whole, unless the snake is too long. When that happens, the roadrunner swallows as much as it can, and then walks around with the rest of the snake hanging from its mouth. As the snake gets digested, the bird gulps down the rest, bit by bit . . . by bit.

From Beeps to Boogers

- Roadrunners live in deserts, mostly throughout the southwestern U.S., including in New Mexico, Texas, Colorado, Arizona, and California.

- Unlike the famous cartoon character, a real road-runner doesn't go *beep, beep*. Like other members of the cuckoo family, its call sounds like *coo, coo*.

- A roadrunner's brown-and-white streaked feathers are a bit drab. That's good news. The bird can blend in with its rocky desert surroundings and avoid becoming dinner. Raccoons, hawks, skunks, snakes, and, yes, those wily coyotes do eat roadrunners. But first they have to spot them . . . and then catch them.

- Male roadrunners don't have bright feathers to attract a female like most other birds. So they bring gifts: a juicy lizard, a field mouse, a bat, or even a scorpion. The male offers the gift to the female and bows. If she likes him, she'll take the gift and gobble it up. Then they'll nest together for life.

- Roadrunners can jump straight up and snatch a hummingbird or a dragonfly right out of the air.

- Roadrunner snot is special. Here's why: Nearly every animal (including you) has to remove excess salt from its body. Most of us do that through our urine. But roadrunners have special nasal glands to do the job. So their snot is salty.

- Desert temperatures can drop below freezing at night. To warm up in the morning, a roadrunner faces away from the sun. It lifts the feathers on the back of its neck to uncover a dark patch of skin. The dark skin absorbs the sun's heat, just like a solar panel.

- It's dry in the deserts where roadrunners live. To conserve moisture, the birds reabsorb the water from their feces before pooping.

• • • • •

That Looney Coyote

Road Runner cartoons and Wile E. Coyote were created by animator Chuck Jones in 1948. He got the idea from a book about the American West by Mark Twain called *Roughing It*. In the book, Twain describes a coyote as "long, slim, sick, and sorry-looking." (Sound familiar?) Twain also says the coyote was hungry enough to "chase a roadrunner." Jones loved that image and created a cartoon around it.

In the cartoons, Wile E. Coyote orders gadgets from the Acme company to help catch the roadrunner. But they always backfire. So in 1990, according to *The New Yorker* magazine, Mr. Coyote filed a lawsuit against Acme. His lawyer told the court that on 85 separate occasions, Acme products caused Mr. Coyote bodily injury, and "restricted his ability to make a living in the profession of predator." The lawsuit was fake, of course, but it's still funny!

Arm in Arm in Arm

Which punch line goes with which joke?

1. ___ What do octopuses hit each other with?

2. ___ What do you call a squid with no eye?

3. ___ Why didn't the squid believe the shark's story?

4. ___ What did the octopus buy at the gag shop?

5. ___ Why wouldn't the shrimp share his dinner with the octopus?

6. ___ What does it take to make a squid laugh?

7. ___ How does an octopus go to war?

8. ___ What do you get when you cross a goat with a squid?

Hello, ladies and jellyfish.

Take my wharf... please.

A. WELL-ARMED **B.** INVISIBLE INK **C.** BILLY THE SQUID
D. HE WAS A LITTLE SHELLFISH **E.** TEN TICKLES (tentacles)
F. SUCKER PUNCHES **G.** IT SOUNDED FISHY **H.** SQUD

Meet the 'Rents

Here's the scoop on which stars got into show biz with a little help from their parents.

Sean Astin

Starred In: *Goonies, Rudy, The Lord of the Rings*
Celeb 'Rents: His dad, John Astin, may be best known as the creepy father on *The Addams Family* television series. Mom, Patty Duke Astin, had her own TV series, *The Patty Duke Show*.

Miley Cyrus

Starred In: *Hannah Montana*
Celeb 'Rents: Dad is country music singer Billy Ray Cyrus. Miley's dad might have been a one-hit wonder with his 1992 single, "Achy Breaky Heart." But then Disney hired him to co-star with his daughter in the Hannah Montana TV series.

Zooey Deschanel

Starred In: *Elf, Almost Famous, The Hitchhiker's Guide to the Galaxy, Bridge to Terabithia*
Celeb 'Rents: Zooey's dad, Caleb Deschanel, was cinematographer for many movies, including *The Patriot* and *The Spiderwick Chronicles*. Mom, Mary Jo Deschanel, starred in the TV series *Twin Peaks*.

Colin Hanks

Starred In: *King Kong* and *My Mom's New Boyfriend* (movies), and *Mad Men* and *Roswell* (TV).
Celeb 'Rents: Dad Tom Hanks is one of Hollywood's biggest stars. Colin's first movie role was a small part in his dad's movie *That Thing You Do!*

Jason Schwartzman

Starred In: *Rushmore, Marie Antoinette*
Celeb 'Rents: Mom Talia Shire played the daughter of Mafia boss Vito Corleone in *The Godfather.* She got the role with help from her real-life brother, Francis Ford Coppola, who directed the movie.

Jennifer Aniston

Starred In: *Marley & Me, Bruce Almighty, Friends*
Celeb 'Rents: Dad is veteran daytime television star John Aniston. He's been playing the same character on the series *Days of Our Lives* since 1985.

Ben Stiller

Starred In: *Night at the Museum, Meet the Parents*
Celeb 'Rents: Stiller got his comedy chops from Mom and Dad. Anne Meara and Jerry Stiller were a husband-wife comedy duo in the '60s and '70s. Now, they often show up in their son's movies.

Victory Dunces

These sports stars prove that winning can hurt.

What a Bonehead. During an NFL football game, Washington Redskins quarterback Gus Frerotte ran the ball in for a touchdown. For some reason, Frerotte celebrated by headbutting the concrete wall behind the end zone. He sprained his neck and had to miss the rest of the game.

Jump for Joy. Baseball player Kendry Morales of the California Angels was at bat in the 10th inning with the bases loaded. He hit a grand slam. The Angels won! After he ran the bases, Morales jumped up and landed on home plate so hard that he broke his leg.

Who Wants a Hug? Kevin Johnson, a star basketball player for the Phoenix Suns, made a game-winning shot at the buzzer. Johnson's teammate, Charles Barkley, ran over and gave him a big hug. Barkley squeezed *so hard* that he injured Johnson's shoulder, sidelining him for the next few games.

Nice Going, Spike. The Pittsburgh Steelers' Plaxico Burress once made a great diving catch. He was so excited that when he stood up, he spiked the football. But no one on the other team had touched him. That meant the play wasn't over. An opposing player picked up the ball, and Burress had to go to the sidelines . . . where his coach was waiting to yell at him.

Dragon Dice

The object is to feed the dragons so they won't eat you. Do that by rolling two dice.

Let's say you roll a 3 and a 4. You could feed dragons 3 or 4—*or* dragon 7 (the dice total). If you roll doubles, you can feed ANY dragon.

Play with others, taking turns. Write your initials on a dragon to show you've fed it. First player to feed all the dragons wins.

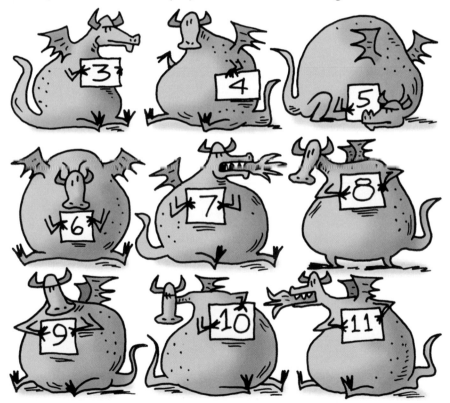

No dice? Toss two coins. Feed any odd-numbered dragon if it comes up one heads and one tails. Feed any even-numbered dragon if both coins are heads. Feed no dragon if two tails are showing.

Make Raisins Dance

Amaze your friends with this simple science trick.

What You Need:

- Small box of raisins

- 1/2 cup clear soda (such as Sprite or 7Up)

- A clear glass

Preparation:

1. Pour the soda into the glass.

2. Drop in a few raisins, one at a time.

3. Watch them do the Funky Chicken (or whatever the current raisin dance craze may be).

The Trick: Raisins "dance" in soda because of *carbonation*. The carbonated water used in soft drinks has gas in it. Carbon dioxide gas, to be exact. The gas makes those little bubbles that sometimes go up your nose. When you drop raisins into soda, bubbles stick to them and they float up. At the top, the bubbles pop. And the raisins drop back down. *Plip, plop! Fizz, fizz!*

Gross Body Facts

Get ready to say, "Eww!"

Munchin' Microbes! Your mouth is at war with itself. Hundreds of species of microbes are fighting each other on your tongue, on your gums, between your teeth—even on that little thing that hangs down in the back of your mouth (your *uvula*). What are they fighting for? The food *you* eat. The microbes want to eat it, too. And some of them even want to eat your mouth! Mostly, your teeth and gums. Thankfully, every time you swallow, millions of microbes are washed down into your stomach. The acid in there destroys them.

Speedy Cells! Right now, millions of cells are crawling around inside you. They have no muscles, bones, or brains. So how can they move? Cells' front ends have thousands of *filaments*—tiny, wiggling hairs. The hairs grab your soft tissue and move the cell forward.

Bulbous Bezoars! Fans of Harry Potter are familiar with *bezoars*. (Harry uses one to save Ron from poison.) Guess what? Bezoars are real. They look like dark, round stones. But they're actually compacted balls of hair, saliva, and other repulsive stuff that collects inside the stomach. They take years to form and can grow as big as baseballs. You need surgery to remove one. The best way not to get a bezoar: Don't eat your hair!

Draw Rollo & Bob

Follow the steps in order.

Sketch in pencil first. When you're happy with your sketch, trace over your lines in ink. Let the ink dry, then erase the pencil lines.

1.

2.

3.

4.

5.

6.

1.

2.

3.

4.

Draw a Rollo & Bob Comic Strip

Add Rollo and Bob to these four comic-strip panels.
Are they standing, walking, sitting? Are they close up
or far away? What are they doing with their arms?

Hey, Rollo. Why are you covered in grape jam?

I wanted to be a jelly roll!

Bob, why is your head in the toilet?

I was feeling flushed.

Come up with your own jokes for these two panels:

Hot Potato

Could hurling a spud end a ballplayer's career?

A Glove Story

Dave Bresnahan was a second-string catcher for a minor league baseball team in Pennsylvania—the Williamsport Bills. He didn't play very often. But on days when the Bills had a doubleheader, he usually played catcher for one of the two games.

The 1987 season was almost over. The Bills had no chance of making the playoffs. Bresnahan was out in the bullpen, where relief pitchers and substitute catchers spend a lot of time, waiting for a chance to play. He was bored. How could he have some fun?

Half-baked Idea

Bresnahan came up with a plan: to use a fake baseball in a game and play a trick on a runner coming into home plate. "It wasn't my intention to do anything undignified," he said later. "But if you've never played in the minor leagues, you don't know about the long bus rides, the low pay, and the tension. If you're not doing well, you could be released at any time. I just tried to liven things up. To put a little fun into a game."

The catcher thought about what he might use. He considered a roll of tape and other objects. "And then it came to me. A potato!" He told some of his teammates about his idea. They thought it was hilarious. But was he brave enough to pull it off?

The Great Tater Caper

The Bills had a doubleheader coming up against the Reading Phillies. For the trick to work, Bresnahan would have to wait for the Phillies to put a player on third base with two outs. Before the game, he peeled several potatoes, and then carved them into balls. "When I plan something out, I make sure the details are covered," he said.

In the fifth inning, a runner made it to third base. Bresnahan told the home-plate umpire that his glove had ripped. He trotted to the dugout for another one: the one with the hidden potato. The Bills who knew what was coming laughed. "Ssh!" he warned.

Back behind the plate, Bresnahan hunkered down. He waited for the pitch, holding the potato in his free hand. When the pitch came, he caught the baseball with his glove. He stood up and threw the *potato* toward third base, as if trying to pick off the runner.

The potato whizzed past the base toward the outfield. The Phillies runner came home. Bresnahan tagged him out, showed the real ball to the baffled umpire, and rolled it toward the pitcher's mound.

The Mashed Potato

The third-base umpire picked up the potato. It had broken into pieces. He yelled to the home-plate umpire to tell him what had happened. The umpire looked at the runner Bresnahan had just tagged out. "Safe!" he called.

Bresnahan was charged with an error. "The umpire didn't have any sense of humor at all," he said.

Throw That Spud Out!

Neither did Orlando Gomez, the Bills' manager. He yanked Bresnahan out of the game. "It was an unthinkable act for a professional," Gomez said. He fined Bresnahan $50.

The Cleveland Indians didn't think it was funny either. (That's the major league team that ran the Bills.) Breshanan was released from the team the next day. His professional baseball career was over. But the potato story became legendary.

A year after his spud caper, Bresnahan was invited back to a Bills' game for "Dave Bresnahan Potato Night." Fans were admitted for $1 . . . and a potato. The Bills sold T-shirts in honor of the event. The ex-catcher even got to re-enact the potato play. And his uniform number, 59, was officially retired by the team.

"Lou Gehrig had to play in 2,130 consecutive games and hit .340 for his number to be retired," Bresnahan told the 4,000 fans who showed up for the game. "All I had to do was throw a potato."

You Name It

Take a minute to memorize each animal's name.
Then turn the page and see if you can write
the correct names under their pictures
(the pictures will be shuffled around).

HARVEY	TAMMY	AMBER
PEABODY	JODIE	BEN
FIFI	MERV	KING

Look on previous
page for answers

DON'T LOOK AT THIS PAGE
UNTIL YOU'VE READ
THE ONE BEFORE IT!

After you've looked at the previous page, go ahead and
try filling in the names. More than half correct is great!

Elephant Jokes

No elephants were harmed in the making of this page (although a few were embarrassed).

Q: Why don't elephants ride bicycles?
A: They have no thumbs to ring the bell.

Q: Why won't African elephants play cards?
A: Because there are too many cheetahs.

Q: What time is it when five elephants are chasing you?
A. Five after one!

Q: What's big and grey and has horns?
A: An elephant marching band.

Q: What did Tarzan say when he saw a herd of elephants wearing sunglasses?
A: Nothing. He didn't recognize them.

Q: What do you call an elephant wearing orange earmuffs?
A: Doesn't matter. He can't hear you.

Q: What do you send to a sick elephant?
A: A "Get Wellephant" card.

Q: Why don't elephants like computers?
A: They're scared of the mouse.

Q: Why are elephants so wrinkled?
A: Have you ever tried to iron an elephant?

Q: How do you make an elephant float?
A: Two scoops of ice cream, root beer, and an elephant.

Gas from Uranus

We Earthlings use a lot of gas to keep our homes warm and our cars running. With our supply running short, where will we find more?

Gas Me Up, Scotty!

The British Interplanetary Society (BIS) has a plan to turn our solar system's biggest planets into gas stations. Why? Because Earth needs a new energy source to run all its gizmos and gadgets.

Four planets—Jupiter, Saturn, Neptune, and Uranus—are full of gas. Not the kind of gas you get from the BP station down the street, but a special gas: helium. Helium makes birthday balloons float, zeppelins fly, and—believe it or not—the Sun shine.

Perfect Planet for a Fill-up

To make large amounts of energy on Earth, we need a certain kind of helium called *helium-3*. Helium-3 can be used as fuel for nuclear fusion, the process that powers the Sun. Fusion could provide all the power Earth needs, but our planet's helium-3 is locked deep beneath the surface. So it can't be used for fuel. Jupiter, Saturn, Neptune, and Uranus—on the other hand—have tons of the stuff just floating around!

BIS studied each planet to see if it would be possible to get gas there. They decided that Jupiter has too much gravity, Saturn has too many rocks in its rings, and Neptune, though in our solar system, is too far away. That leaves . . . Uranus!

To Uranus or Bust

Designs have already been made for a high-speed, nuclear-powered space freighter that would take just 70 days to reach Uranus. Once it arrived, the main ship would launch smaller ships, called probes, into the planet's atmosphere. These would release floating robotic mines to collect gas.

A ship could be on its way to collect gas from Uranus as soon as 2100. The scientists working on the project don't know if their plan will ever be carried out. And, if it is, they don't know if it will succeed. But trying and failing and then trying again is how scientists learn.

Flubbed!

Wacky headlines from real newspapers

Helicopter Powered by Human Flies

Trees Can Break Wind

Yellow Snow Studied to Test Nutrition

Astronauts Practice Landing on Laptops

Eye Drops off Shelf

Mystery at Mystic Seaport

It's fun to tell ghost stories by flashlight,
but what if a haunting turned out to be real?

Who Ya Gonna Call!

On a rainy spring night in 2006, five researchers brought flashlights and cameras aboard the *Charles W. Morgan*. The 165-year-old ship—America's last surviving wooden whaler—is docked at Connecticut's Mystic Seaport. The team's mission: hunt for ghosts.

Three different people had seen a man on the *Morgan* dressed in old-fashioned sailor's clothes. He was smoking a pipe. He nodded but did not speak.

The seaport museum invited the Rhode Island Paranormal Research Group to search the ship. Why? Sailors—like the one people had seen—once worked in the ship's blubber room. During long sea voyages, they cooked down whale blubber in huge pots to make oil. But the *Morgan* made its last voyage in 1921. No (living) sailors could possibly be aboard.

A Whale of a Ghost Story

The *Morgan* made 37 voyages in search of whales between 1841 and 1921. Most journeys lasted about a year, but some lasted five years. About 30 sailors were aboard for each trip and around 1,000 sailors worked on the *Morgan* at one time or another during its 80 years of whaling.

When ghost hunter Renee Blais searched the ship, she felt the presence of 15 men. She thought they had been aboard the whaler during a powerful storm at sea. She felt a sense of "sickness, death, and despair." Were these sailors' ghosts still aboard?

Creep Me Out

Dawn Johnson, a museum guide for the *Morgan*, said she hated to go belowdecks alone at night. "It is creepy down there. It's cold and clammy. You hear moans and creaking, and you wonder what it is."

Andrew Laird, founder of the paranormal research group, says that 90 percent of the time, his team finds a natural explanation for scary sounds. Sometimes it's an animal making the noises. Or the sounds turn out to be the normal sounds a building (or ship) makes. The *Morgan* was different.

On the *Morgan*, the ghost hunters felt presences "on every deck of the ship." So they decided to return with more equipment. They brought infrared cameras, microphones, and electromagnetic field detectors, a device that tracks energy shifts. "If a gnat jumps, we'll know it," said Laird.

And they did. Down in the blubber room, the detector's needle began to swing back and forth. The device buzzed like a mosquito. Laird, who says he has seen only two ghosts in his lifetime, claims to have seen one aboard the *Morgan*. "Do I think it's haunted? Yes!" he said.

Fish Tale

Ever had a big one get away? Not like this!

One evening in 1867, Dr. Frank Buckland spotted a 212 pound sturgeon at a fish seller's shop near his home in England. He asked to borrow the fish for the night so he could make a plaster cast (a copy) of it for his fish museum. He promised to have the fish back by no later than 10 a.m. Here's what Buckland says happened when he (and the fish) got home.

Tying a rope to his tail, I let him slide down the stone stairs. He started all right, but I could hold the rope no more. Away he went sliding headlong down the stairs. He smashed the door open, and slid right into the kitchen. At last he brought himself to anchor under the kitchen table.

This sudden and unexpected appearance of the armor-clad sea monster created a sensation. The cook screamed, the housemaid fainted, the cat jumped on the dresser, the dog retreated behind the copper and barked, the monkeys went mad with fright, and the sedate parrot has never spoken a word since.

A copy of the sturgeon did make it into Buckland's Museum of Economic Fish Culture. It was one of 400 plaster casts on display. Why all those plaster fish? Dr. Buckland wanted to create a love of *pisciculture.* That's fish breeding . . . in case you wondered.

Rotting Flesh

Become a zombie without that icky smell.

What You Need:

- 1/2 cup instant oatmeal
- 1 tablespoon flour
- Bowl
- Spoon
- Red food coloring
- Green food coloring

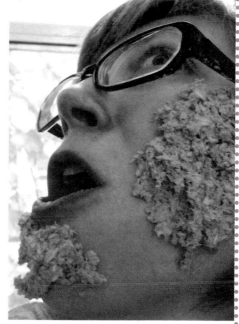

Preparation:

1. Combine the oatmeal, 2 tablespoons of water, and one drop each of red and green food coloring in a small bowl. Stir the mixture, adding more water if needed to make a thick paste. (If the paste gets too thin, thicken it with a small amount of flour.)

2. Drip in more food coloring if you want your flesh to look especially bloody or gangrenous.

The Prank: Smear generous amounts of the oatmeal "flesh" on your face and arms. Give it a few minutes to dry, then sneak up behind your victim and start moaning.

Answers on page 276

It's a Zoo in Here!

Identify each animal, then write the word in the proper spot on the next page, one letter per box. We put in ELK at 3-Down to get you started.

1
2
3
4
5
6
7
8
9
10
11
12
13
14
15
16
17
18
19
20
E
L
K

Bonus: Unscramble the letters in the yellow boxes to answer this joke: **What animal has four legs and flies?**

Lifesaving Kids

Fictional heroes have big muscles and wear capes. But as these stories prove, real-life heroes come in all sizes . . . capes are optional.

Cool Cub!

In 2009, 10-year-old Kyle Forbes learned CPR with his Cub Scout troop in Houston, Texas. Kyle is autistic, which affects how his brain processes information. So that night, his dad worked with him to make sure he fully understood the training. He did.

A few days later at school, Kyle's art teacher, Sheri Lowe, started choking on an apple. There was no one else in the classroom, so Kyle rushed over and squeezed her from behind. But she was still choking!

"I got it, Mrs. Lowe," Kyle calmly reassured her. Remembering his lesson, he adjusted his position and squeezed her again. The apple chunk popped out, and Mrs. Lowe could breathe. Today, she calls Kyle her hero. "He saved my life."

Clever Caller

Alana Miller was at home playing with her mom, Erika, in Oak Harbor, Washington, in 2007. Suddenly, her mom stopped playing. She stumbled a few steps, and fell face-first on the floor. Alana tried to see if her mom was OK, but she wasn't moving. So Alana got Erika's cell phone, dialed 9-1-1, and said two words: "Mommy owie." That's all it took. A few minutes later, paramedics came into the house and found Alana putting a blanket over her mother, who was still unresponsive. They took Erika to the hospital. It turned out that she had suffered a severe migraine headache. Doctors aren't sure what would have happened if help hadn't arrived so fast. What's most amazing about this story? Alana's age. She was only two years old!

Super Swimmer

In the summer of 2009, 12-year-old Neal Simon was riding his bike at a campground in Honey Brook, Pennsylvania. Neal heard someone calling for help, and when he looked out at the lake, he saw a man struggling in the water. Neal had recently completed a water lifesaving course. Though he weighed barely 70 pounds, Neal swam out and pulled the grown man to safety.

The man, 53-year-old Howard Anderson, had been fishing in his canoe when it turned over. Anderson's feet got caught in underwater weeds, and he wasn't a good swimmer. "No one else was there," Howard said. "If it wasn't for Neal, I would have drowned."

Neal said it wasn't that big of a deal—he was just in the right place at the right time. Most people at the campground were surprised when they heard about Neal's bravery. Why? Because until then, he had been known in the camp as a "little troublemaker."

Not-So-Super Superheroes

We've taken some ordinary words and turned them
into superheroes. Match them up, then make your own.

1. BALL GIRL
2. BAT BOY
3. COUNTRYMEN
4. COWGIRL
5. DOORMAN

6. LUNCH LADY
7. MAILMAN
8. SALESWOMAN
9. SUPERSTAR
10. GARBAGE MAN

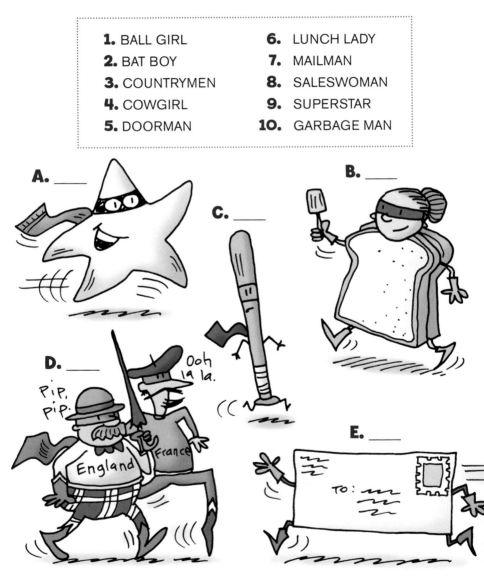

DO-IT-YOURSELF:
Try drawing a superhero with a name that fits. Supermarket? Snowman? Flower girl? Busboy? Use a separate piece of paper if you need more room.

F. ____

G. ____

H. ____

I. ____

J. ____

Hairstory

Orange and blue hair? Old-fashioned? Yep!

The First Punks

When the Saxons invaded Britain 2,500 years ago, they went to battle with hair and beards dyed orange, green, bright red, and blue. Why? To scare the enemy. In case that didn't work, they also carried two-handed battle-axes that could cut a horse in half.

The Red Queen

Back in the late 1500s, Queen Elizabeth I's red hair sent the English into a hair-dyeing frenzy. Men and women of the court wanted to show their loyalty to the queen. So they dyed their hair (some men even dyed their beards) to match the queen's hair color. Loyalty came with side effects. The dye they used—a mix of saffron and sulfur powder—caused nausea, headaches, and nosebleeds.

Where do pilots dye their hair?

Rainbow Brite

In the early 19th century, people darkened their hair or beards with a form of silver called *lunar caustic.* (We call it silver nitrate.) Indoors, lunar caustic made hair look black. In bright light, it made hair (and beards) shimmer with rainbow colors . . . sort of like a pigeon's neck or a rooster's tailfeathers.

Wacky Ways to Color Your Hair

(After you get your parents' permission . . .)

Kool-Aid: A packet of unsweetened Kool-Aid mixed with a tablespoon of conditioner equals colorful hair that smells fruity. Separate out the hair you want to color and coat with the mix. Put on a plastic cap to keep in moisture. Leave color on for 6 to 10 hours (or overnight), then rinse thoroughly. Kool-Aid dyes hands, ears, faces, and clothes, too. So use gloves, put Vaseline anywhere the mix might touch skin, and wear old clothes.

Tea: To tint hair red, rinse it with tea made from rose hips or Red Hibiscus.

Potato Water: To darken hair, boil unpeeled potatoes. Let the water cool, and then use it to rinse your hair.

At the hairport!

Food Coloring: Put colorful highlights in blond hair using food-coloring paste. Separate out a strand, coat it with paste, and then cover with foil. Leave on for an hour, or overnight for more vivid color.

Washable Markers: Choose a marker and use it to highlight strands of hair. Color washes out in one shampoo.

Buggy Race

Pick a bug and start running. One rule—no backing up!
If you don't make it to the end, pick another bug and start
over from the beginning. How many bugs did you use?

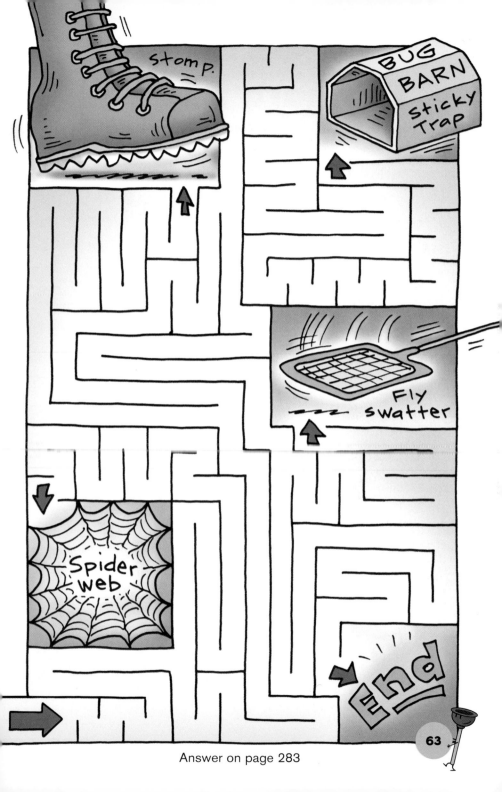

Stomp.

BUG BARN Sticky Trap

Fly swatter

Spider web

End

63

Answer on page 283

Die-hard Hot Dog

Here's the story of the toughest wiener on Earth.

Pranked

The strange tale of the Die-hard Hot Dog (DHHD) began on July 4, 2001, with a simple act of clumsiness. A guy named Josh Severin dropped a hot dog off the grill. Feeling pranky, he stuck it on the antenna of his father-in-law's truck. Severin didn't let on that he'd done anything. He just kept asking, "What did you do to your truck?"

Finally, his father-in-law, Richard Carroll, spotted the hot dog. It looked goofy on top of the antenna. But he decided to leave it there, not knowing it would become the DHHD!

Indestruct-i-dog

More than ten years later, the hot dog was still around. It survived snow, rain, bitter cold—and three pickup trucks. (Carroll moved it to the antenna of each new vehicle he bought.) It even survived a huge hail storm. In 2008, the truck got pounded—broken windows, a bunch of dents—$4,000 worth of repairs. But the DHHD survived.

Today, the hot dog has shriveled into a gross, black, crusty thing about the size of your little finger. Carroll is reluctant to get rid of it. He figures someday he may cremate it . . . probably on a grill.

Answers on
page 277

Brain Buzzers

Beware of tricks in these three brain-buzzing questions!
Can you figure out each one?

1. A turtle and a slug run a 10-yard race. The turtle wins, with the slug making it only 5 yards. They race again, but this time the turtle starts 5 yards farther back (he has to run 15 yards to the slug's 10 yards). Who wins?

2. It takes a drop of newt spit 80 seconds to evaporate under a hot lamp when the mad scientist is wearing her white lab coat. When she doesn't wear the coat, it takes a minute and 20 seconds. Why is this? (The amount of spit and heat are identical.)

3. In a standard deck of playing cards, there are 4 queens, 4 kings (one that's one-eyed) and 4 jacks (two that are one-eyed). How many total eyes are there on these 12 cards?

The Pirate Bride

*Here's a story you may not have heard about
Blackbeard, the most famous pirate of them all!*

Hornswaggled

Tales abound of Blackbeard's deeds in the Caribbean,
but he also sailed up to New England. Around 1715,
some say, Blackbeard brought a treasure ship to the
tiny Isles of Shoals near New Hampshire. One of his
crewmembers was a lady pirate. He took her ashore
and married her. Then—so the story goes—Blackbeard
and his bride went to Smuttynose Island for a
honeymoon. He left her there to guard the buried
treasure, and went in search of more loot.

Pirate's Dozen

Three years later, Blackbeard was dead—done in by
the British Navy in a bloody sea battle. But what of
his wife? She was still on Smuttynose Island.

Rumor has it, Blackbeard had at least a dozen
other wives. Maybe he simply forgot where he'd left
this one. She waited on that lonely island until her
death, 17 years later. As for the treasure: Some say
she guards it still.

Ghosts, Ho!

Few people live on the Isles of Shoals. Those who do
swear that spooks haunt the islands. Blackbeard's

bride is one of the best known. Some claim to have seen her: a milky-white ghost standing on a point of land overlooking the Atlantic. Others say they've heard her whisper "He will return" over and over. They say she watches for his ship, certain that he has not abandoned either of his treasures: his pirate booty or his pirate bride.

Blackbeard himself now haunts the rocky Isles of Shoals. At least, that's what the islanders say. (Maybe they're hoping a few ghost hunters will show up to keep them company.) As for Blackbeard, if he's trying to find his lost bride, he's about 300 years too late. And the treasure? It has never been found.

Riddle Me Timbers!

1. How much does it cost a lady pirate to get her ears pierced?

2. What's the first thing a lady pirate does if she falls overboard?

3. What do you get when you cross a lady pirate with a zucchini?

4. What color is bad luck for pirates?

5. What do you call a lady pirate with a sword?

6. Where is the ladies' room on a pirate ship?

Answers on page 277

The Bangkok Café

These menu items might look fake, but trust us, they're real. You can order these dishes at restaurants all over Thailand—if you dare.

Menu

Appetizers

- Deep-fried scorpions
- Boiled silkworm cocoons
- Pan-fried buffalo dung beetles

Salad

- Ground-frog salad
- Duck salad (served with or without duck's blood)
- Noodle-jelly salad

Main Course

- Fried beef gums
- Grilled pig's tail
- Crickets in coconut cream
- Vegetable curry with ant eggs
- Grilled duck's beak

Words & Giggles

Some words are just more fun than others.

Too Funny to Eat. Comedian George Carlin had a few things to say about food words—like *guacamole*. "That sounds like something you yell when you're on fire," said Carlin. "Guacamole!" As for garbanzo beans, Carlin pointed out that it starts with the same letters as *garbage*. "Hey, did you take out the garbanzo beans?"

Dilbert's Computer. Cartoonist Scott Adams writes the lines for Dilbert, the character who makes fun of working in office cubicles. In one comic strip, Dilbert's computer gives him a list of the world's funniest words: *chain saw*, *prune*, and *weasel*.

A Presciption for Funny. Dr. Robert Beard, also known as Dr. Goodword, has hundreds of words he thinks are hilarious. His list includes *yahoo*, which meant "a country bumpkin" way before it was the name of a search engine. And *turdiform*, which means "like a songbird," not . . . well, that other thing that probably came to mind.

The Original Goonies. In 1951, two young comics named Spike Milligan and Harry Secombe launched *The Goon Show*. Up to nine million Brits tuned in each week to hear words that made sense twisted into words that . . . didn't. "We'll all be murdered in our tigers!" the funny men cried. "Ying tong iddle-i po!"

Bird-Poop Pancakes

Gross out your family by downing one of these goopy pancakes.

What You Need:

- Griddle or frying pan
- Large bowl
- 2 small bowls
- Spatula
- Microwave
- Zip-top bag
- Scissors
- Plate

Ingredients:

- 1 tablespoon butter
- 1/2 cup pancake mix
- 1 1/2 tablespoons chocolate chips
- 10 mini marshmallows

Preparation:

1. Melt the butter on the griddle over medium heat. Stir the pancake mix together with the amount of water specified on the package, and drop the batter onto the griddle in three or four lumps.

2. Sprinkle 1 tablespoon of chocolate chips on the pancakes while they cook. Let the pancakes cook for about two minutes before flipping them with the spatula.

3. While the pancakes are cooking on the second side, put remaining 1/2 tablespoon chocolate chips in a small bowl. Melt them for about 30 seconds in the

microwave. Stir the melted chips until smooth, and then scoop them into a bottom corner of a zip-top bag. Cut off a very small part of the corner.

4. As the pancakes finish cooking, put the mini marshmallows in the second bowl. Microwave them for 10 to 15 seconds.

The Prank: Put the hot pancakes on a plate. Using your zip-top pastry bag, pipe a bird footprint onto each pancake. Plop the melted marshmallows near the bird tracks and pipe little drops of chocolate on top of them. Then put the plate near an open window. Show everyone the surprise a bird left on your pancakes. Then chow down!

Altamaha-ha

You've probably heard of the Loch Ness Monster, the sea serpent said to lurk in a lake in Scotland. But have you heard about its cousin? It lives about 250 miles from Atlanta, Georgia . . . or so we've been told.

Hiss-story

The Altamaha River winds through 137 miles of Georgia's hardwood and longleaf pine forests. It cuts through rice fields and feeds cypress swamps. At the end of its journey, the river empties into the Atlantic Ocean near Brunswick, Georgia. Along the way, it gathers more than just water. It gathers tales.

More than 200 years ago, the Tama Indians described "a huge water serpent that hissed and bellowed" living in the Altamaha River. The Tama (a little-known tribe with ties to the Creek Indians in Florida and Alabama) no longer live along the river's banks. But sightings of the Altamaha-ha continue to this day.

Taking the Bait

Details about the sea serpent differ from witness to witness, but Donny Manning's story is typical. One July night in the late 1960s, Donny and his brother were trolling for catfish on the Altamaha River. Suddenly, something grabbed their bait—a clay-like mixture of oatmeal and soda. Donny said it was not a catfish or a sturgeon, both common fish in the Altamaha. He'd hauled in plenty of those before. This time, he'd snagged a gun-metal gray creature 10 to 12 feet long with a snout like an alligator and a tail like a dolphin. It snapped Donny's 40-pound test line like kite string and disappeared.

Close Encounter with Alfie

In May of 1998, three young swimmers decided to beat Georgia's sweltering summer heat. They headed for the Altamaha River to take a dip. Rusty Davis and Owen Lynch watched from the dock as their friend, Bennett Bacon, jumped into the river.

"Then this thing popped out of the water," Rusty told a reporter from the *Brunswick News*. "It was gray and brown, and it had stuff all over it, like seaweed and grass." And the "thing" was only ten feet away from Bennett.

Rusty and Owen screamed for their friend to come back to the dock, but he thought they were kidding. Then he turned around, just as a dolphin-like tail plunged beneath the murky river water.

The three boys were sure they'd seen the famous river monster. Georgia state wildlife officials suspect eyewitnesses don't really see the Altamaha-ha. Perhaps they see manatees: large, gray, saltwater mammals sometimes called "sea cows." But most eyewitnesses are locals. They insist that they know the animals common to the river. And a gun-metal gray sea serpent is not one of them.

British Oops!

*Two true stories of grown-ups
goofing up in Great Britain.*

Sour Flowers

Beware the poisonous purple monkshood flower!
Sure, it's pretty, but it's also one of the deadliest
flowers in the world. (Just touching the plant can
cause suffocation.) That's why town officials in
Kendal, England, were embarrassed in 2011 when
they learned that they had accidentally planted purple
monkshoods next to a children's playground. (A local
gardener noticed them and alerted the officials.)
Thankfully, the flowers were removed before any kids
ate them.

Planetary Distress Signal

One night in the town of Tynemouth, England, a man
saw a bright light floating in the sky near the beach.
He thought it was an emergency signal flare that had
been fired by someone on a ship. Fearing the ship
was in trouble, the man called the police. The British
Coast Guard sent out several helicopters and rescue
boats. They searched the coastal waters for hours
looking for signs of a ship in distress, but couldn't
find anything, so they finally gave up. The next night,
the man saw the "signal flare" again. That's when he
realized it was actually . . . the planet Jupiter.

Answers on
page 277

Shape Shifting

The two shapes in the box can fit together to make five of
the eight figures on the page (without rotating the two shapes).
Which three figures CAN'T they make? We colored the J shape
blue in the first one to show you how they were fit together.

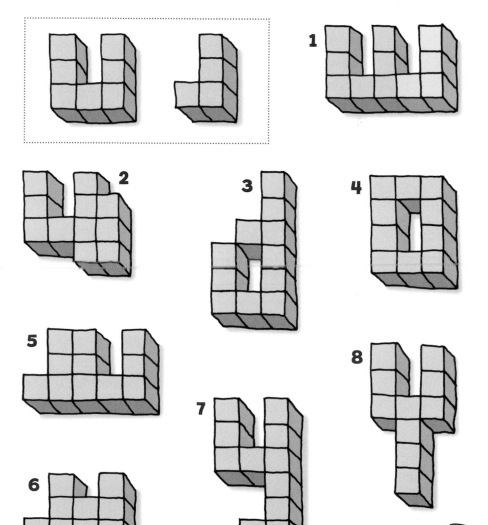

Odd Jobs

Still wondering what to be when you grow up?

Be an ... Eiffel Tower Painter! Gear up like a mountain climber and crawl all over the most famous tower in the world. It takes 18 months, 60 tons of paint, and 1,500 brushes to paint the 986-foot-tall tower. Caution: Some say paint is the only thing keeping the tower from falling down.

Be a ... Raisin Inspector! Watch raisins pass by on a conveyer belt. The key to a job well done? Pull apart any raisins that are stuck together. (Yawn.)

Be a ... Cat-Food Tester! For every batch of cat food, you'll perform three quality-control tests. Test 1: Stick your face in a tub of cat food and take a big sniff. Is it fresh? Go to Test 2: Plunge your arms in up to the elbows, feel for bony bits, and take them out. Got all the bones out? Go to Test 3: Smear a big glob flat and prod it with your fingers to check for gristle. If it's gristle-free, you're done.

Be an ... Ant-Farm Supplier! Capture ants for toy ant farms. First, stick a soda straw into an anthill and blow through it until ants start pouring out. Scoop up the ants and seal them in a jar before they get away.

Be a ... Drive-Through Safari Guard! Sit at the exit and watch for animals trying to escape. Keep a close eye on the monkeys. They like to hitch rides on top of cars. Your job: Shoo them off with a stick.

Answer on page 277

Figure It Out

These two stick figures have a mystery riddle for you. Just fill in the letters to finish what the girl stick figure is saying. That will help you get the answer—and explain why they like that letter.

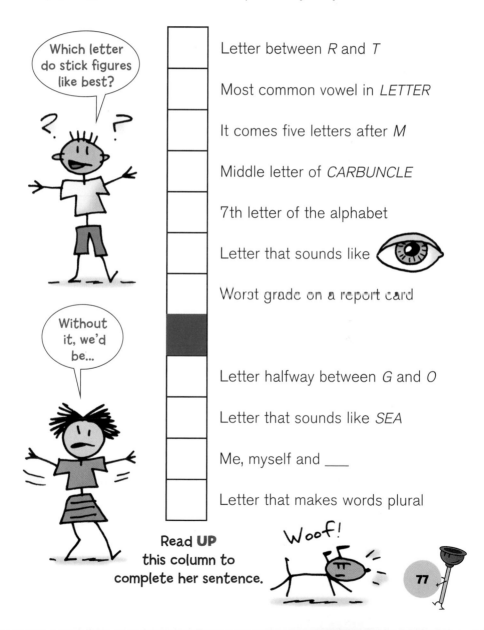

Which letter do stick figures like best?

Without it, we'd be...

Letter between *R* and *T*

Most common vowel in *LETTER*

It comes five letters after *M*

Middle letter of *CARBUNCLE*

7th letter of the alphabet

Letter that sounds like

Worst grade on a report card

Letter halfway between *G* and *O*

Letter that sounds like *SEA*

Me, myself and ___

Letter that makes words plural

Read UP this column to complete her sentence.

Woof!

77

The Fastest Men on Two Wheels

Feeling sluggish? Rev up with motorcyle racing.

Fast

Glenn H. Curtiss was a bicycle racing champ, but no matter how fast he went on a bike, it wasn't fast enough. So Curtiss added engines to the Hercules bicycles his company made. He turned them into custom-made motorcycles built for one thing: speed. On January 23, 1907, Curtiss showed the world what he and his 40 horsepower, 4,000 cubic centimeter, V-8 powered machine could do. He roared down the hard-packed sand of Ormand Beach on Florida's east coast. And he reached a then jaw-dropping top speed of 136.3 miles per hour. That earned Curtiss the title "The Fastest Man on Earth."

Faster

In 1962, New Zealander Burt Munro was determined to fulfill his life's dream—to race his home-built 1920 Indian motorcycle on the Bonneville Salt Flats in Utah. The problem: Munro was 63 years old, and he had a bad heart. Some scoffed at the idea that he could truly compete. Munro had another problem: He lived in New Zealand, and it would cost a lot of money to get himself and his Indian to Utah. Munro scrimped and saved. He traveled to the United States on an old cargo ship, working as a cook to pay his way.

When Munro finally lined up his Indian at the starting point on the blinding white Utah salt flats, he was there to win. He cranked up his bike to 178.97 miles per hour. The bike's muffler got so hot, it burned the flesh right off his leg. But that didn't stop him. Munro blew away the competition and set a record.

Back on the salt flats in 1967, Burt set another record for an Indian motorcycle—190.07 miles per hour. "We were going like a bomb," he said. "Then she got the wobbles just over halfway through the run. To slow her down I sat up. The wind tore my goggles off, and the blast forced my eyeballs back into my head. I couldn't see a thing." Burt Munro's life inspired the 2005 movie *The World's Fastest Indian*.

Fastest

Forty-nine years later Bill Warner headed to a runway at Loring Air Force Base in Maine. He hopped on a turbocharged 1,299cc Suzuki Hayabusa motorcyle and blasted off. Within seconds, Warner had become the first person to ever pass 300 mph on two wheels. His record-breaking speed: 311.945 mph.

To put that into perspective, Japan's high-speed bullet trains have a top speed of 217 miles per hour. Warner would have left a bullet train in the dust. But he had to stop . . . before the runway ended. "The bike was bouncing, hopping, skipping, and sliding," Warner said. "It was a little scary." He had a mile to stop, and it took every inch of it.

Fairy Dusting

This pixie has been hard at work sweeping up the fairy dust in the basement of her tree house. Can you trace the path she swept from START to END?

Start

End

Hollywood Chills

Where do stars go after they die?
Some prefer to stay in Hollywood . . . forever.

Star-studded Cemetery

Since 1899, famous actors, musicians, directors, writers, and producers have been laid to rest in a palm-shaded Hollywood cemetery. Its name: Hollywood Forever. More stars are buried there than anywhere else on Earth.

From the cemetery's front gate, you can see the Hollywood Hills and the famous Hollywood sign. Inside, marble monuments and tall old-fashioned headstones cast creepy shadows across the lawns.

Lights, Camera—BOO!

Believe it or not, people come to this cemetery at night. And not to visit the graves. They come to watch movies, such as *Suspiria*, a horror film about a coven of witches. The films are projected onto the side of a white marble mausoleum. And when a film ends, one source says, "The walk out is a little spooky."

That's not the only spooky thing that happens at Hollywood Forever. In the 1920s, Paramount Studios purchased 40 acres from the cemetery to build a back lot. Studios once did a lot of filming on back lots. They built elaborate sets, sometimes whole city streets, to film TV shows and movies.

Some swear that Paramount's back lot is home to more than just film sets. Strange noises have been heard—knocks and disembodied footsteps. People have seen a ghostly woman who smells of roses and a spectral man dressed all in white. Perhaps the spirits of stars buried in Hollywood Forever are still waiting for their cues.

Fangs for the Memories

Here are some of the creepier tales about stars buried at Hollywood Forever.

Star: Clifton Webb (1889–1966)
Haunted History: Actor Clifton Webb lived in a Beverly Hills mansion with—so he claimed—the ghost of an opera star who had once lived there. And she wasn't the only one who didn't want to move on after death. A few days before a heart attack ended Webb's life, he told his psychic, "I'm not leaving this house, even at death."

It seems he wasn't kidding. The new owners said Webb haunted his old armchair by causing weird noises when anyone sat in it. Bathroom toilet paper unrolled by itself. And, more than once, someone used the bathroom but . . . didn't flush.

In the 1990s, the mansion was torn down, so the star's ghost moved on . . . to Hollywood Forever Cemetery. His shade has been seen pacing the marble corridor of the mausoleum that houses his body. For some reason, Webb's ghost smells of cologne.

Star: Rudolph Valentino (1895–1926)
Haunted History: At age 31, complications from
surgery sent silent-film star Rudolph Valentino to an
early grave. Fans were heartbroken. At least 3,000
people gathered at the cemetery for his internment. A
plane dropped rose petals from the sky. And then, all
of the mourners left . . . or did they?

On the first anniversary of Valentino's death, a
woman dressed all in black visited the cemetery. Her
face was hidden by a heavy black veil. She placed a
bouquet of red roses at Valentino's crypt. And then
she left as quietly as she had arrived. The Lady in
Black shows up every year on the anniversary of the
star's death. No one knows who she is. But she
always leaves roses.

Star: Maila Nurmi (1922–2008)
Haunted History: Nurmi's gravestone at Hollywood
Forever is a bit . . . different. It is engraved with a
picture of the star dressed in a long, figure-hugging,
black dress. She is standing between a spider-web
curtain and a candelabra. And the name "Vampira" is
chiseled beneath her feet. Why?

Because, in the 1950s, Nurmi was TV's first late-
night horror movie host. Fans loved her blood-
curdling scream, her deathly pale skin, and her long
blood-red fingernails. And they loved the way she
ended each show: "Unpleasant dreams, darlings."

Meet more Hollywood Forever stars on page 236.

Answer on
page 277

Mystery Joke

There's a joke below. Can you figure out how to read it?
When you do, you should be able to find the answer as well.

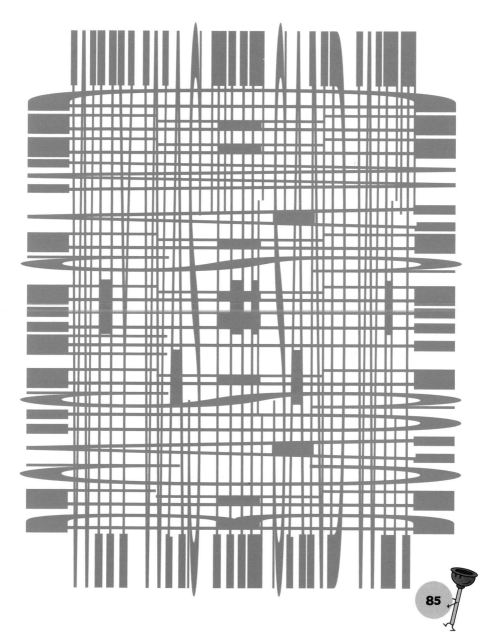

85

Dumb Crooks

Here's proof that crime doesn't pay.

Grab-Bag Surprise

When a purse snatcher mugged an 86-year-old woman in Netley Abbey, England, he got a big surprise. The woman was walking her dog. Inside her handbag: the contents of her pooper scooper.

To Infinity! (And Jail)

A thief stole a Buzz Lightyear toy and hid in the bushes from the officers chasing him. They might have passed him by, but . . . Buzz was a talking toy. As police hurried past, he bellowed: "Buzz Lightyear! Permission to engage." The officers engaged, all right. They hauled the thief off to jail.

Man of Steal

A shoplifter at an Ohio Wal-Mart stuffed some DVDs into his shirt and started to run. He didn't get far. Employees had been watching him all along. Why? He was dressed as Superman.

Unchecked Baggage

A German man spent 14 weeks in jail and paid a $3,540 fine after being being arrested at a New Zealand airport. He was trying to smuggle 44 lizards out of the country . . . in his underwear.

Yay! Rats!

Each answer contains the word *RAT*, so we've drawn a rat
where those three letters go. Fill in the rest of the letters
to answer each clue. For example, the first one is *BRAT*.

1. Badly behaved kid: B __

2. G, PG or PG-13: __ __ __

3. Hole in the moon made by a meteorite: __ __ __

4. *The* __ *Kid* (a movie): __ __ __

5. Robber at sea with an eye patch: __ __ __

6. Use your nails on an itch: __ __ __ __

7. A baby's noisy, shaking toy: __ __ __ __

8. What "O" on a phone stands for: __ __ __ __

9. 26-mile running race: __ __ __ __

10. Opposite of a Republican: __ __ __ __ __

Extra Credit:

11. Focus and
think hard: __ __ __ __ __ __ __

Catacombing

*You've played hide-and-seek. But have you
played it in the dark, seven stories below ground?*

Tour de Dead

Deep beneath the streets of Paris, the catacombs
await. Dark. Some say haunted. And filled with the
bones of six million people. Visitors can (legally) enter
only one part of this underground maze: the Ossuary,
a mile of tunnels and underground rooms stacked
with skulls and femurs and tibias and spines. A sign
over the entry reads "Stop! This is the Empire of the
Dead." But with a ticket for the tour, it's OK to enter.

Into the Cheese

Beyond the Ossuary lies a 1,900-acre maze that
started with . . . a bathroom. Around 2,000 years ago,
the Romans invaded France. (It was called Gaul
then.) Once the Romans reached Paris, they seriously
needed baths. They carved limestone from the
ground to build them, and left behind quarries and
tunnels. Miles and miles of them.

When the Romans left, the French wanted more
than just baths. They dug up limestone to build
monuments like Notre Dame cathedral and the
Louvre museum. Over time, they dug tunnels for
sewers and subways, water pipes and parking
garages. They ended up with layer after layer of
tunnels, some only 15 feet below ground, others as

deep as 120 feet. Parisians call this multilevel hole-filled maze *gruyére*. (That's French for Swiss cheese.)

Sneaky Cats

The catacombs have 180 miles of tunnels. That's about the distance from New York City to Baltimore, Maryland. Subtract the part that is open to the public—the Ossuary—and you have 179 miles of tunnels that are "off limits." To expore this part of the catacombs, you have to break the law.

Enter, the *cataphiles*. That's what the French call people who explore forbidden parts of the underground maze. The *cats* of Paris sneak into the catacombs through manhole covers. Or they find forgotten tunnel entrances in the basements of churches, hospitals, skyscrapers, and schools. Why? Because these cats love deep, dark adventures.

On the Prowl

To keep their identities secret, cataphiles go by code names like "Painted Lizard," "Yopie," and "Crato." Just like real cats, they roam around at night.

Under cover of dark, they climb down long rickety ladders to get to lower levels. Sometimes, they have to tromp through sewage. Why slog through poo? "At the surface there are too many rules," says Yopie. "Here we do what we want."

Some cataphiles create art. One carved a castle into the limestone wall of a quarry. It had a drawbridge, moats, and towers. A little LEGO soldier guards the gate. Some like to give parties. An author and an artist hosted a candlelit book party for their graphic novel, *The Green Devil*, in a secret underground room. Some just explore, like the cat who wears scuba gear and dives feet first into icy abandoned wells.

Catacops

Enter at your own risk! Most tunnels are pitch-black. It's easy to get lost. Sometimes tunnels collapse. A whole neighborhood got swallowed back in 1961. So the city hired *cataflics* (catacops) to keep people out.

As the catacops patrol the tunnels, they learn the secret twists and turns of the maze. When they find someone lurking down there, they escort them back to street level and make them pay a fine. Then they let them go. Of course, many scurry right back to the tunnels as soon as the sun sets.

Good Cat, Bad Cat

The first Chief Catacop, Jean-Claude Saratte, thought there were two kinds of cataphiles: those who just loved exploring the catacombs and those who went underground to cause trouble. He went after the troublemakers. (The "good" cats helped find them.)

When Chief Saratte retired, the cataphiles threw a huge party for him. They had fire-eaters, food, and music—in a gallery deep beneath the city streets. "I tried for years to catch you." The chief grinned. "Now I'm retiring. If you want, you can take pictures with me." Everyone did.

The Cats Guide to the Underground

*Here's the gear you'd have to wear
and some sights you might see if you
COULD explore the catacombs.*

Catagear: Waterproof knee-high boots. Scruffy jeans. A hoodie. (It's a chilly 55 degrees down there.) And a miner's helmet for light. (It's dark!)

Catasights:

- *The vault containing the gold reserves for the entire country of France.* Inside, you'd find 2,600 tons of gold: stacks and stacks of bars in tall steel cages. And each bar is worth half a million dollars!

- *The watery lair of the* Phantom of the Opera. Though the phantom is a writer's creation, the water below the Paris Opera House is real. It bubbles from the ground all the time into a huge stone water tank. The tank keeps the cellar from flooding. Eerie white catfish swim there, and opera employees feed them.

- *The beach.* It's not really a beach. It's an underground room. One cataphile painted a wave rolling across a wall, and other cats hauled in buckets of sand to cover the floor. What's under the sand? Bones, or so the rumors say.

- *The WWII Nazi bunker.* The German military turned one quarry into a hidden headquarters, 70 feet below ground. The bunker had a kitchen, a shower, and even toilets! There's a lot of gunky brown stuff in those. Rust, we hope.

Fake Cocoa Spill

If you really want to drive your parents bonkers, this is the craft to do!

What You Need:

- 1 teaspoon nontoxic brown paint
- 1 1/2 tablespoons white glue
- Paper or plastic cup
- Marshmallow
- Wax paper
- Spoon

Preparation:

1. Mix the paint and glue together in the cup until all the swirls are gone. Lay out a piece of wax paper, and pour the mixture out of the cup and onto the paper. Lay the cup on its side at the end of the spill, and place the marshmallow in the center of the spill.

2. Let the spill dry on the wax paper for at least 48 hours. When it's completely dry, peel the spill and the cup off the wax paper.

The Prank: Place the spill, complete with cup, in a high-traffic area of your home. Then sit back and enjoy the show.

Tooth Traditions

In the U.S., the Tooth Fairy takes kids' teeth from under their pillows and leaves money. Here's what to do if you lose a tooth in other countries.

Mexico. Put the tooth in a box on the bedside table and wait for *El Raton* (a magical mouse) to visit. *El Raton* will take the tooth and leave money. (He leaves more money for a front tooth!)

Costa Rica. Forget the Tooth Fairy. Just have a jeweler dip the tooth in gold. Then have your gold-plated teeth made into earrings.

South Africa. Leave the tooth in a slipper. That night, a mouse will take the tooth and leave a gift in its place. Make sure to check your slippers for mice before sticking your feet into them again!

Morocco. Put the tooth under your pillow. Early the next morning, throw it toward the sun and shout, "I give you a donkey's tooth and ask you to replace it with a gazelle's tooth." If you ignore the tradition, your new tooth will look like a donkey's tooth.

Turkey. Have your parents bury the lost tooth in a place related to what you want to do in the future. If you want to be a doctor, have them bury the tooth near a hospital. If you want to write for Uncle John's Bathroom Readers just . . . go with the flow!

Go, Banana Slugs!

Check the college football or basketball results, and you'll see lots of Wildcats, Knights, Bulldogs, Lions, and Panthers. Dozens of teams are known by those names. Here are some of Uncle John's favorite one-of-a-kind team names.

- Anteaters (University of California-Irvine)
- Banana Slugs (University of CA-Santa Cruz)
- Bloodhounds (John Jay College of Criminal Justice, NY)
- Blue Hose (Presbyterian College, SC)
- Fire Ants (University of South Carolina-Sumter)
- Gophers (Goucher College, MD)
- Hardrockers (South Dakota School of Mines)
- Humpback Whales (University of Alaska-SE)
- Manatees (State College of Florida)
- Minutemen (University of Massachusetts)
- Moose (University of Maine at Augusta)
- Peahens (Saint Peter's College, NJ)
- Pilgrims (New England College, NH)
- Railsplitters (Lincoln Memorial University, TN)
- Thundering Herd (Marshall University, WV)
- Ducks (University of Oregon)

Team Name Trivia

• There are more than 60 school teams called the Eagles, but only Lock Haven University of Pennsylvania has a team known as the Bald Eagles.

• Lots of schools call themselves the Bears, but only the University of Maine is specific enough to be the Black Bears. There are at least six Golden Bears, three Grizzlies, and five Bruins. Livingstone College of Salisbury, NC, goes by the Blue Bears.

• Sixteen colleges have stingers: 9 Yellowjackets, 6 Hornets, and 1 Bee. And two have fangs: Rattlers and Cobras.

• Plenty of schools want the power of nature behind their teams, including Texas A&M (Dustdevils), the University of Miami (Hurricanes), and SE Oklahoma State (Savage Storm).

• Some of the most famous nicknames belong to teams that have had a lot of athletic success. You've probably heard of the Alabama Crimson Tide, North Carolina Tar Heels, Nebraska Cornhuskers, Arkansas Razorbacks, Notre Dame Fighting Irish, and the Indiana Hoosiers.

• Seventeen schools want to fight it out, but their names might not help them win, including the Fighting Quakers, Fighting Camels, Fighting Blue Hens, and Fighting . . . Artichokes.

Answer on
page 277

Wacky Whazzits

Drawing tricks have been used to create these impossible
objects—except for one! Which one do you think could
really exist? Find out how to make it on page 260.

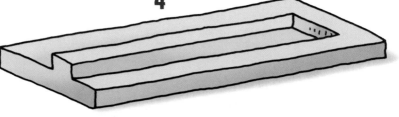

1

2

3

4

5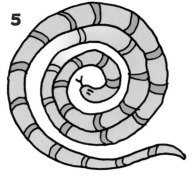

6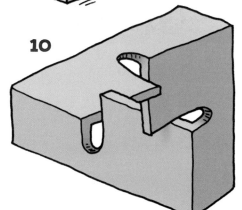

7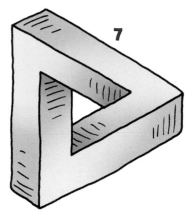

8

9

10

And: Try drawing some of these yourself—or better yet, make up your own impossible objects.

Stand-up Folks

These comedians will crack you up.

"Dogs have no money. Isn't that amazing? They're broke their entire lives. But they get through. You know why dogs have no money? No pockets."
— Jerry Seinfeld

"People always ask me, 'Were you funny as a child?' Well, no, I was an accountant."
— Ellen DeGeneres

"I come from a very big family . . . nine parents."
— Jim Gaffigan

"Changing a diaper is a lot like getting a present from your grandmother: You're not sure what you've got, but you're pretty sure you're not going to like it."
— Jeff Foxworthy

"Mom always said, 'Keep your chin up.' That's how I ran into the door."
— Daryl Hogue

"My childhood was a blur. I needed glasses."
— Wendy Liebman

"Moms can get so mad they forget your name. 'Come here, Roy, er, Rupert, er, Rutabaga . . . what *is* your name? And don't lie to me, because you live here, and I will find out who you are.'"
— Bill Cosby

"Some people are afraid of heights. Not me, I'm afraid of widths."
— Steven Wright

"When I was born I was so surprised, I didn't talk for a year and a half."
— Gracie Allen

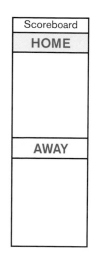

BASKET

Penny Basketball

1 POINT

1 POINT

Place a penny on one of the brown circles or in the yellow area. Put a finger on the penny, close your eyes, then slide it toward the basket. Stop and open your eyes.

A penny completely in the basket (not touching the red rim) scores the points from where you started. Play to 20.

2 POINTS

2 POINTS

2 POINTS

Try using a nickel… or a quarter!

3 POINTS
shooting from anywhere in the yellow area

Talking Blues

*If songwriters can play
with words, so can we!*

If I Had a Hi-Fi

In 1965, a folk singer named Bob Dylan recorded a
song called "Subterranean Homesick Blues." He used
a singing style called "talking blues." Talking blues
sounds like fast, rhythmic speaking . . . with a tune.
Dylan wrote serious songs about civil rights, war, and
being young in a mixed-up world. But he used
strange rhymes:

> **Better jump down a manhole**
> **Light yourself a candle**
> **Don't wear sandals**

Dylan made a short film to promote "Subterranean
Homesick Blues." In the film, he stands in an alley
wearing a plain black vest over a button-down shirt.
The song plays in the background. Dylan keeps a
stern face as he flips over cards with rhymes from
the lyrics:

> **Bad Cough, Paid Off**
> **Fleet Foot, Black Soot**
> **Short Pants, Romance**

In 1993, *Rolling Stone* magazine ranked Dylan's
"Subterranean Homesick Blues" film number seven in

a list of "100 Top Music Videos." That's pretty good, because when Dylan made his song promo, no one had even *heard* of music videos. (MTV wouldn't be around for another 15 years.)

Never Odd or Even

In 2003, comedy singer Weird Al Yankovic decided to have some fun with Dylan's film. He wrote his own version of "Subterranean Homesick Blues." But instead of rhymes, Weird Al used palindromes.

A *palindrome* reads the same forward and backward. Every phrase in Weird Al's song was a palindrome, even the title, "Bob" (Dylan's first name). Al used single-word palindromes (*noon, level, pep*) and palindrome phrases (*UFO tofu, lemon a melon*). He even used sentences, which are much trickier:

Do geese see God?
A dog, a panic, in a pagoda.
Oozy rat in a sanitary zoo.

Too Hot to Hoot

Weird Al's video recreated the scene from Dylan's film. He dressed like Dylan, wore a curly wig to look like Dylan, and stood in an alley. He kept a stern expression on his face, just like Dylan. As he flipped over cards with his palindromes on them, he sang in the "talking blues" style. Al's spoof was a hit. So were his palindromes!

Palindromania!

Now it's your turn to go word-crazy.

To create a palindrome, look for words with a lot of vowels. Also look for letters that appear often, such as *n, s, r,* and *t.* Start with easy words and build from there. This palindrome sentence has five simple words, and each of the words is a palindrome, too:

Did Dad poop? Dad did.

Some palindromes are simple statements: *Madam, I'm Adam.* Really clever palindromes make a comment: *Elk rap song? No sparkle.* See if you can finish the palindromes below by filling in the blanks.

1. Bombard a _ _ _ _ mob.

2. Race fast, _ _ _ _ _ car.

3. Step on no _ _ _ _ _ .

4. _ _ _ _ _ _ at a spool.

5. Toot. A moody baby _ _ _ _ _ . A toot!

6. Do nine men interpret? _ _ _ _ _ _ _ _ , I nod.

Bonus: Find what is hidden in the purple headlines of "Talking Blues" (on the previous page).

Answers on page 278

Palidrome Generator

Create your own palidromes in the space below.
The chart will give you a start.

dud	gig	a	eye	solos	civic	toot
mom	wow	level	did	gag	sos	redder
bib	ewe	pup	tot	kayak	Otto	sees
now won		but tub		pot top		
was saw		pets step		rats star		
dumb mud		flex elf		yo bozo boy		
pee weep		Dr. Awkward		drowsy sword		
taboo bat		Neil an alien		llama mall		

The Royal Sillies

Sometimes you have to be a bit bonkers to rule a kingdom. Or maybe just refuse to grow up.

- Nabonidus, King of Babylon from 556 to 539 BCE, ate grass. He thought he was a goat.

- Rome's Emperor Nero (37–68 BCE) sent runners high into the Alps to find snow. They had to race all the way back *down* the mountains before the snow melted. Why? Nero wanted his favorite treat: fruit-flavored snow ice cream.

- Queen Christina of Sweden (1626–89) really hated fleas. So she had a four-inch-long cannon made and shot tiny cannonballs at them.

- Think you hate baths? King Louis XIV of France (1638–1715) never took a bath. Not one. Ever.

- King Philip V of Spain (1683–1746) thought he would die if he changed his clothes. So he didn't. Instead, he wandered around his palace in rotting rags. He thought the tattered clothes were the only things holding him together.

- Emperor Ferdinand I of Austria (1793–1875) liked to wedge his bottom in a wastepaper basket and roll around the floor.

- England's Queen Victoria (1819–1901) loved dogs. Her first royal act was to bathe her favorite dog. She kept up to 83 pet pups in Buckingham Palace and knew each one by name. Her Scottish sheepdog, Noble, stood guard over her gloves when she stayed at Balmoral Castle in Scotland.

- Queen Henriette of Belgium (1836–1902) had a pet llama. She trained the royal pet to spit on commoners.

- The castle built by King Ludwig II (1845–86) in his Bavarian kingdom inspired Disney's Sleeping Beauty Castle. Castles cost a lot of money. To pay for his, Ludwig planned a few bank robberies. When that didn't work, he tried to sell Bavaria. His ministers put him under house arrest to keep him out of trouble.

- Prince Henry (1900–1974), Queen Elizabeth II's uncle, once kept King Olav of Norway waiting for half an hour. Why? The prince couldn't tear himself away from the *Popeye* cartoon he was watching.

- England's King George VI (1895–1952) gave his daughter Elizabeth a Corgi named Dookie. When the king phoned his daughter long distance, she ended the calls with a "good-bye" bark from Dookie.
  In 1953, Princess Elizabeth became Queen Elizabeth II. Though Dookie has passed away, four other Corgis share Buckingham Palace with the Queen. And the royal chef prepares their meals. On the menu: poached chicken, rabbit, or beef.

Which Liquid?

What's going to come out of the hose below?
Pick a barrel and follow its hose. If it doesn't lead
to the two kids, try another. (You can go under hoses.)

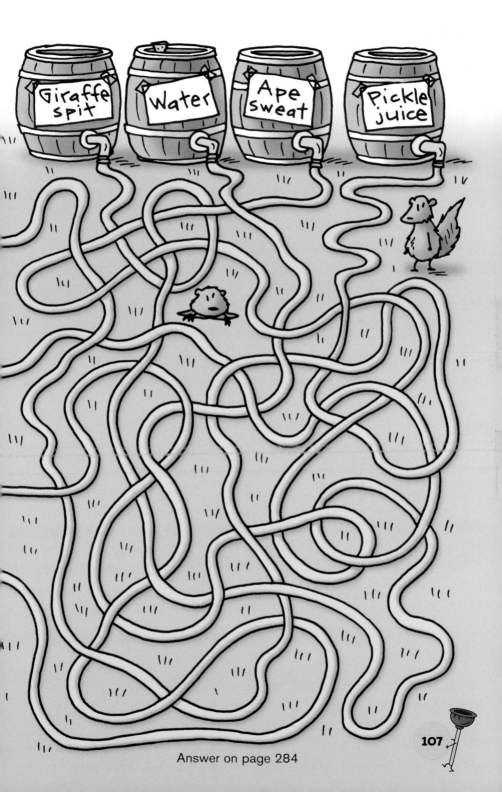

Answer on page 284

The Hunting of the Snark

Author Lewis Carroll wrote about some weird creatures. These verses are about one of them.

"We have sailed many months, we have sailed many weeks,
　　(Four weeks to the month you may mark),
But never as yet ('tis your Captain who speaks)
　　Have we caught the least glimpse of a Snark!

"We have sailed many weeks, we have sailed many days,
　　(Seven days to the week I allow),
But a Snark, on the which we might lovingly gaze,
　　We have never beheld till now!

"Come, listen, my men, while I tell you again,
　　The five unmistakable marks
By which you may know, wheresoever you go,
　　The warranted genuine Snarks.

"Let us take them in order. The first is the taste,
　　Which is meagre and hollow, but crisp:
Like a coat that is rather too tight in the waist,
　　With a flavour of Will-o'-the-wisp.

"Its habit of getting up late you'll agree
　　That it carries too far, when I say
That it frequently breakfasts at five-o'clock tea,
　　And dines on the following day.

"The third is its slowness in taking a jest.
　　Should you happen to venture on one,
It will sigh like a thing that is deeply distressed:
　　And it always looks grave at a pun.

"The fourth is its fondness for bathing-machines,
　　Which it constantly carries about,
And belives that they add to the beauty of scenes—
　　A sentiment open to doubt.

"The fifth is ambition. It next will be right
　　To describe each particular batch:
Distinguishing those that have feathers, and bite,
　　From those that have whiskers, and scratch.

"For, although common Snarks do no manner of harm,
　　Yet I feel it my duty to say,
Some are Boojums—" The Bellman broke off in alarm,
　　For the Baker had fainted away.

• • • • •

So . . . What's a Boojum Anyway?

Here are three definitions.

1. A secret supersonic nuclear missile (MX775B Boojum) developed by the U.S. in 1946.

2. A tree shaped like a spiny upside-down carrot that grows in the Sonoran Desert of Baja California.

3. A kind of snark. It causes any who meet it to "suddenly vanish away, and never be met with again."

Life in Potterland

Here's what the Harry Potter stars have to say.

"I've spent half my life playing the character Hermione Granger. I was 9 years old in the first movie. I was still losing baby teeth."

–Emma Watson
(Hermione Granger)

"I read all the Harry Potter books. When I was about 10, I said to my mom, 'If they make a film, will you take me to go see it?' Little did I know that I'd be in it!"

–Matthew Lewis
(Neville Longbottom)

"There was lots of roiling about and sword fights in *The Chamber of Secrets*, so it was great."

–Daniel Radcliffe
(Harry Potter)

"When they started burning down the Room of Requirement, it got very, very hot. We were climbing huge mountains of chairs and desks and boxes. I've never been so frightened in all my life."

–Tom Felton
(Draco Malfoy)

"I sit on a broomstick for hours, and it hurts. It gives me a numb bum."

–Rupert Grint
(Ron Weasley)

"Hermione uses all these big long tongue-twister words. I don't know what she's going on about half the time!"

–Emma Watson
(Hermione)

"While shooting the scene where we jumped off a dragon into a lake, we got pulled out of the water because it was so cold Rupert turned purple."

—Daniel Radcliffe
(Harry)

"It's unbelievable seeing me as an action figure! Just think. Toddlers all around the world will be biting my head off!"

—Emma Watson
(Hermione)

"Luna was a lot more scary than Voldemort. Girls in general are scarier than Voldemort."

—Matthew Lewis
(Neville)

"I once played a trick on the makeup people. I put a fake-blood capsule in my mouth, and then pretended to trip on the stairs and let the blood pour out. They really fell for it! Then they chased after me with a water pistol."

—Daniel Radcliffe
(Harry)

"What a house. Turns out they're doing OK, the Malfoys. However, the interior decorating leaves a lot to be desired. And needless to say, Voldemort isn't the greatest houseguest."

—Tom Felton
(Draco)

"The last day of filming was kind of like the last day of school. I took home all these odd birthday cards and toys that I'd collected over the years."

—Rupert Grint
(Ron)

Face-Crook

Click here if you *like* it when criminals get caught because they goof up on Facebook.

● A Pennsylvania woman returned home one day to discover that someone had broken into her house. Her diamond rings were gone. She panicked. Then she looked at her computer and felt better. Why? It was open to the Facebook page of her teenage neighbor. He logged on while he was robbing the house and then forgot to log off. He was arrested.

● After a masked man robbed a bank in Houston, Texas, police had no leads. But then someone (police don't know who) sent them a link to 19-year-old Ricky Gonzalez's Facebook page. There was a photo of him holding lots of money. His status: "I'M RICH!" Not for long. Detectives soon discovered that Ricky was friends with one of the bank's tellers. She had helped him plan the robbery. They were both arrested.

● A British burglar named Craig Lynch escaped from a minimum-security prison. Police couldn't find him . . . until he started taunting them on his Facebook page. Lynch posted status after status about how much "fun" he was having. By looking at his updates, police were able to figure out where Lynch was hiding. He was re-arrested. Now he's locked up in a *maximum*-security prison . . . with no Internet access.

Answer on
page 278

Ship's Wheel of Fortune

What has 12 legs, 12 arms and 12 eyes?

Arr, mateys, here's how to find the answer:

Start at the arrow. Write that letter in the first space below.

Continue around the wheel in the direction shown, writing down

EVERY OTHER letter (you'll have to go around the wheel twice).

Answer: ___ ___ ___ ___ ___ ___ ___ ___

___ ___ ___ ___ ___

That's Zedonk-ulous!

*Animal hybrids aren't just science fiction.
They're real. Check these out to see for yourself.*

Natural Hybrids

Animal hybrids happen when one species (or subspecies) of animal mates with an animal of a different species. "Natural" hybrids aren't planned. They happen when two species living in the same area mate and produce offspring.

Zebra + Donkey = Zedonk Caretakers at the Chestatee Wildlife Preserve in Dahlonega, Georgia, thought nothing of letting their donkeys pasture with their zebras. They figured it was impossible for them to breed. But two zedonk babies proved them wrong. The hybrid foals have donkey-brown bodies and zebra-striped legs. And they've become a popular attraction at the p--reserve.

Grizzly + Polar Bear = Pizzly As people move into areas that were once wilderness, grizzly bears get pushed farther and farther north. Most now live in Alaska and Canada. Result: They come in contact with polar bears. Grizzlies and polar bears are both part of the brown bear family. Their cubs have fur that looks white like a polar bear's with patches of brown fur like a grizzly's. They also have the grizzly's long claws and humped back. Scientists theorize that global climate change helped the two types of bear get together. Melting Arctic ice makes it warm enough for grizzlies to survive the frozen winters in polar bear country.

Narwhal + Beluga = Narluga The narwhal is a porpoise found in Arctic waters. It has a long, straight ivory tusk that led to its nickname: "the unicorn of the sea." Belugas are medium-sized whales that also live in Arctic waters. In the 1980s, scientists found the skull of a narwhal-beluga hybrid near Greenland. The find worried scientists. Hybrids are often infertile—they can't reproduce. Narwhals and belugas are among 22 species in the far north in danger of extinction due to hybridization.

Hybrids by Design

People create animal hybrids for specific purposes. Some scientists think there should be laws for crossbreeding. They worry that a "mad scientist" might decide to create animal-human hybrids. Don't laugh. Researchers in Britain have considered injecting human genes into primate brains, just like in the movie *Rise of the Planet of the Apes*.

Cattle + Buffalo = Cattalo Kansas rancher Charles Jesse "Buffalo" Jones first bred cattalo in 1886 after a brutal blizzard froze thousands of head of cattle solid. Jones lassoed a few buffalo calves and brought them to his ranch to mix with his cattle. He hoped to create a long-haired hybrid that could survive against the cold prairie winters. Unfortunately, Jones's cattalo were mostly infertile. Today's beefalo are the result of similar crossings, begun in the 1970s. Beefalo can survive harsh winters and produce healthy calves.

Camel + Llama = Cama Camels can be cranky. They bite and spit, and they can be hard to handle. But they are still one of the most popular modes of transportation in Middle Eastern deserts. Scientists at the Dubai Camel Reproduction Center created the cama: a camel-llama hybrid. First born in 1998, camas are easier to get along with, have no humps, and produce more wool for weaving cloth.

Lion + Tiger = Liger If you mate a male lion with a female tiger, you'll create cubs that grow to be the biggest cats in the world. Dr. Bhagavan Antle, director of South Carolina's Institute of Greatly Endangered and Rare Species, says that female lions and male tigers have an "inhibitor growth gene." That's a gene that keeps lions and tigers from growing too big. But when you cross a female tiger and a male lion, the inhibitors disappear. Ligers grow to be more than ten to twelve feet long and weigh up to 900 pounds. That's the size of the mother and father combined.

What Do You Get?

These crossings are just for laughs!

Q: What has a tiger's stripes, a toucan's beak, a giraffe's neck, and a baboon's bottom?
A: A zoo.

Q: What do you get if you cross a pig with Count Dracula?
A: A hampire.

Q: What do you get if you cross a baby with a UFO?
A: An unidentified crying object.

Q: What do you get if you cross a compass and a shellfish?
A: A guided mussel.

Q: Cross a rubber baby buggy with a rainstorm?
A: You get a rubber baby buggy dumper.

Q: What do you get when you cross a bear and a skunk?
A: Winnie the P-U!

Q: What do you get when you cross a Cuban dance with an elephant?
A: Mambo jumbo.

Q: What do you get if you cross a cow with a waiter?
A: A cow that wants to be tipped.

Q: What do you get when you cross a humpbacked bear with an iceberg?
A: A grizzly *brrr!*

Q: What do you get if you cross an earthworm with a cyborg?
A: The Worminator.

Whangdoodle Wednesday

Sense or nonsense? Try to figure out the meaning before you check the definitions.

One Wednesday, I saw a **whangdoodle** sitting outside my school. He kept wiping his beak with a tissue. After a few minutes, he picked up a **sackbut** and played a few sad notes. *Phew!* The air coming from that horn smelled like skunk spray. That whangdoodle had a horrible case of **ozostomia**.

I felt bad for the little guy, so I offered him half of my peanut butter and jelly sandwich. He almost fell off the steps. I guess whangdoodles have **blennophobia**. I had to tell him over and over that the stuff on the sandwich was just green apple jelly.

He sat there for a minute, all **rigidulous**. Then he relaxed, took a bite, and smiled. A few minutes later, I wished I hadn't shared. Peanut butter gives whangdoodles **ventoseness**. And there's nothing worse than a sackbut-blowing ventose whangdoodle!

DICTIONARY

BLENNOPHOBIA: a morbid dread of slime
OZOSTOMIA: really bad breath
RIGIDULOUS: stiff
SACKBUT: an instrument similar to a trombone
VENTOSENESS: a tendency to fart
WHANGDOODLE: a mythical bird that cries a lot

Roll 'em!

Here are three *other* things to do
with a roll of toilet paper!

Roll Rolling: Clear the area in front of a wall, at least six feet away, and see who can roll a toilet-paper roll closest to the wall without touching it. If everyone touches the wall in a round, no one wins. Try again.

Mummy Arms: Check with the toilet-paper buyer in your house to see if one roll can be spared. If so, start wrapping the toilet paper around each arm and hand. Keep your thumbs separate, like mittens. When you're done, hold your arms out in front of you as you walk. Ta-da: Mummy Arms!

Sheet Walking: Tear off a strip of toilet paper 10 sheets long. Lay the strip on a table and place the roll at one end. Lift the empty end of the strip off the table (you can hold both ends yourself or have a friend hold one end). Now, slowly raising the end with the roll, try to "tightrope walk" the roll all the way to the other end. It's not easy. Try longer strips.

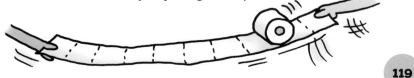

You Smell!

At least, you might . . . if you eat a certain green veggie. Here's the story.

That's Asparagusting

Benjamin Franklin said a lot of wise things in his life. This bit of wisdom was a little odd: "A few stems of asparagus eaten shall give our urine a disagreeable odor." Across the ocean in England, a gentlemen's club agreed. A sign posted outside the club read, "During the asparagus season, members are requested not to relieve themselves in the hat stand."

In more modern words, eating asparagus makes your pee stink. Why? Like its vegetable relatives—onions, garlic, and leeks—asparagus contains sulfur. Sulfur is what makes eggs, cheese, feces (poop), and even skunk spray so smelly. And it smells a lot like rotten eggs. Sulfur is also known to cause bad breath and stinky farts.

When your body breaks down the sulfur in asparagus, it goes to your kidneys for waste disposal; in other words, it becomes part of your pee. When you urinate, the sulfurous odor drifts up to your nose. And . . . pee-ew!

Smell What?

Except—some people *can't* smell it! Researchers at the Monell Chemical Senses Center in Pennsylvania study the senses of taste and smell. In 2010, they brought 38 adults to the center. Why? They wanted to find out which ones could smell asparagus pee.

Test subjects visited the lab two different times to pee in jars. The first time, scientists asked them to *not* eat asparagus for 24 hours before giving a urine sample. Then—after they'd peed in jars—each person was given asparagus to eat. Two hours later, they all peed into clean jars.

The test subjects came back to the lab on another day to sniff the urine samples—their own and those of other people. They had to smell a few samples at a time, to prevent "nose fatigue." Most of the test subjects could smell the asparagus odor, but six percent could not.

My Genes Smell Better than Yours

Next, the researchers swabbed cheek-cell samples from each person. They wanted to see if there was a gene that let some people smell asparagus in urine. The result? There *is* an "asparagus pee gene." Having that gene helps a person sniff out the odor.

Neuroscientist Marcia Pelchat thinks the asparagus pee smell may be "a bouquet of aromas." (Yum!) So more tests are needed. Pelchat isn't worried about finding test subjects. "Luckily, we have a very good asparagus recipe, so people are willing to participate," she said.

Want to take the Stinky Pee Test? See page 180.

Toilet Terror!

Most toilets are perfectly safe.
(We think.)

Exploding Head. At a Washington, D.C., office building in 2011, a worker excused herself to go to the restroom. When she was done, she flushed. And then . . . BOOM! Everything in the toilet went *out* instead of in. The toilet seat burst into tiny pieces, and the woman ended up in the hospital. Management blamed "high air pressure in the water system." The victim recovered. But she'll never forget her flush—er . . . brush—with death.

Kat & the Rat. Kat Selvocki was watching a movie in her New York City apartment when a huge rat ran across the floor. Freaked out, Kat grabbed a broom and searched her apartment. She didn't find the rat. But she found clues to how it got in: water splashes on the bathroom floor and rat hair in the toilet.

Wild Ride. A worker at a nuclear power plant in Washington was using an outdoor portable toilet. It started to shake violently. He was thrown this way and that. Stuff splashed *everywhere*. When the ordeal ended with a thud, the worker tried to open the door to flee. It was stuck. So he yelled for help, and *that's* when the forklift driver realized someone was inside. He'd been told to move the portable potty 20 feet, and was just doing his job. (Oops.)

Complete the Comic

A Rollo and Bob comic strip awaits you on the next page—BUT FIRST, you need to come up with nine words that'll finish it off.

1. a type of insect (plural): _____

2. a dish you'd have for dinner: _____

3. any kind of liquid: _____

4. a plant (plural): _____

5. a type of pet: _____

6. a TV show: _____

7. a sea creature: _____

8. an illness: _____

9. something sold in a grocery store:

_____

Complete the Comic

Insert the words in order from the previous page.

Tingue Twusters!

Say these out loud (really *loud*).

- How many clams can a man cram in a clam can?

- Sixty-six sick chicks kick sixty-six slick sticks for kicks.

- Red leather yellow leather red leather yellow leather.

- Bored Bill and a bored bird bored into a board in bored Bill's billboard, and the bored bird got billed for the board bored into bored Bill's billboard!

- Which Swiss watch did which Swiss witch wear, and which Swiss witch wore which Swiss watch?

- Extinct insects' instincts stink.

- Mix-master Max mixed biscuit mix—briskly.

- Big bad bedbugs bug bigger bedbugs to beg big baggers to bag even bigger bad bedbugs!

- Rapping rabbits wrap radishes in radish wrappers.

- Theodore Thistle threw three thorny thistles. How many thorny thistles did Theodore Thistle throw?

- I thought a thought, but the thought I thought I think was not the thought I thought. The thought I think I thought was not.

On the Line

Two teen heroes give a new twist to "catching the big one."

Help, Eh?

The July day in 2011 started off warm and sunny. But by late afternoon a breeze came up, turning Lake Erie's waters choppy. Two buddies, 14-year-old Danny Park and 15-year-old Alex Humphrey, were doing some fishing at Waverly Beach. The beach is on the Canadian side of Lake Erie, just across the bridge from Buffalo, New York.

Just as the sun began to set, an 8-year-old American boy who was fishing nearby dropped his rod into the water. And then he made a big mistake: he went in after it. Within seconds the rough water pulled him away from shore.

"He can't swim!" the boy's father yelled as he jumped in after him. Then the boy's grandmother waded in to try to help.

Alex and Danny watched in horror as the choppy water sucked the whole family out . . . farther and farther from shore. "They were yelling at us," Danny said. "Panicking."

An Erie Sight

"The waves were quite big—three or four feet," Alex said. "They kept getting pushed out. I thought they were going to die."

Danny and Alex were locals. They had been fishing these waters for a long time. They knew that if they swam into the dangerous waves to save the family, five people might drown instead of three. So they got creative. Alex bit the lure off the end of his fishing line. Then he tied his line to Danny's fishing pole, pulled back, and cast Danny's pole toward the struggling family.

The rod flew through the air and landed close to the boy. Alex braced himself, getting ready to reel in whatever he caught. "The kid grabbed onto Danny's fishing rod, and I pulled him in," Alex said. Then Danny grabbed the kid and dragged him onto the shore.

Reel Lifesavers

The two teenagers rescued the father and the grandmother the same way—using one pole to cast the other pole within reach. One at a time, they pulled the father and grandmother to safety without endangering their own lives. "If we had gone in to help them, I think we all would have drowned," said Danny. "It's really rough water."

Thanks to Alex and Danny's quick thinking, the three Americans survived their ordeal with just a few scratches.

Watch Out for the Piranha!

This fishing game is sure to hook you.

Object of the Game: Three paper people are treading "water" in a cardboard box. The water is filled with friendly perch and hungry piranha. Your job is to rescue the people without getting gobbled up.

Number of Players: Play alone or with a friend.

Preparation: To make your fishing pole, find a stick about three feet long. (A yardstick will do.) Cut a 36-inch length of string. Tape it firmly to one end of the fishing pole. Tape a magnet to the free end of the string—that will be your hook.

Draw the outlines of 3 people, 10 perch, and 5 piranha on a sheet of paper. Cut out the shapes and slide a paper clip onto each one.

How to Play: Toss the folks and fish into a box and shake to scramble the catch. Cast your line and win points for each shape you catch: people are worth 10 points; perch are worth 5. But if you catch a piranha, you *lose* 5 points . . . or a few fingers! The player who earns the most points by the time the people have all been rescued wins the game.

Cyclops for Breakfast

Gobble it up before it stares you down!

What You Need:

- Drinking glass
- Toaster
- Frying pan
- Spatula

Ingredients:

- 1 slice of bread
- 1 teaspoon butter
- 1 egg

Preparation:

1. Press the rim of the drinking glass firmly into the middle of the piece of bread. Wiggle it around to make sure it cuts all the way through. Then pop out the bread circle. Put the bread circle in the toaster while you melt the butter in the frying pan.

2. Place the piece of bread in the frying pan, and crack the egg into the bread hole. Let the egg cook over medium heat for a few minutes until the yolk is no longer soft.

3. Tear Cyclops "eyebrows" and a big fat nose off your toasted circle, place them on the creature, and dig in!

Dino Who?

*Here are the stories of three dinosaurs
that had scientists fooled . . . for a while.*

Hey, Jonesi!

About 112 million years before Texas became a
state, dinosaurs called the place home. How do we
know? Because dinosaur tracks and bones litter the
Jones Ranch in the center of the Lone Star State.
At first, the Texas dinosaur was thought to be a
Pleurocoelus (PLOOR-oh-SEEL-us). The bones of
this 60-foot-long plant eater were first found in the
late 1880s in Maryland.

In 1997, the Texas state legislature dubbed
Pleurocoelus the official state dinosaur. "It's our
dinosaur, by golly, and we're Texans, so we're going
to be proud of it," wrote Texan Clay Coppedge. But
in 2007, Dallas dino expert Peter Rose took a closer
look at the Texas bones. They did *not* match those
found in Maryland. Turns out, Texans can be prouder
than ever. Their dinosaur is a brand new species,
and it has a new name: *Paluxysaurus jonesi*
(pu-LUHK-see-SORE-us JONES-ee).

A Bum Raptor

Picture a chicken the size of a nine-year-old kid, with
tiny clawed hands and a few feathers sprouting from
its wings. A sci-fi movie monster? Nope. A raptor that
lived about 80 million years ago. *Oviraptor* (oh-vee-

RAP-tor) was first discovered in Mongolia's Gobi desert in 1923. Its bones were found near broken eggshells believed to belong to another dinosaur. So it was given a name that means "egg thief." For 70 years, scientists thought *Oviraptor* swiped and ate the eggs of other dinosaurs.

Then, in 1993, dinosaur hunter Mark Norell went to the Gobi Desert. He found a fossilized *Oviraptor* hunkered down atop a nest with its arms folded over the eggs. It reminded him of a chicken brooding on a nest. Norell noticed that the top of one egg had worn away. Inside, he found a surprise: the skeleton of a baby *Oviraptor*. The "egg thief" wasn't stealing eggs. It was guarding its own eggs from danger. Norell nicknamed the raptor "Big Mama."

Off with Its Head

Who wouldn't love getting a package in the mail full of dinosaur bones? In 1868, Dr. Edward Cope got so excited about the three dinosaur vertebrae shipped to him by a fossil hunter in Kansas that he asked for more. The next shipment contained 900 pounds of dinosaur bones!

Cope put the bones together and decided that the long-tailed beast was a new kind of plesiosaur. He named it *Elasmosaurus platyurus* (ee-LAS-mo-SORE-uhs plat-ee-YOOR-uhs). Then another scientist showed up and pointed out that what Cope had thought was the dinosaur's long tail was really . . . its neck. Cope had stuck the dinosaur's head at the wrong end.

The Word Museum

*Next time you need a word to bamboozle
your friends, dust off one of these!*

Bombilate: To hum or make a buzzing sound.

Cabobble: To mystify, puzzle, or confuse.

Eldritch: Weird.

Fanticles: Freckles that look like small ticks.

Gloppened: Surprised.

Idle-worm: A lazy person.

Jargogle: To mess up.

Kiddliwink: A small village shop.

Lumbricoid: Like an earthworm.

Mumblecrust: A toothless person.

Olla-podrida: Leftovers.

Quaggle: To quiver like jelly.

Sandillions: Numbers as high as grains of sand on a beach.

Undercold: A cold caught from the ground.

Vomitory: A big door to let crowds leave a building.

Wamble: A stomach gurgle.

Xanthodont: Yellow teeth, like a rat's.

Yird-swine: A frightful animal thought to haunt graveyards and eat dead bodies.

Zowerswopped: Bad-tempered or crabby.

Turkey Talk

Match up these jokes and punch lines, and then write
them in the word balloons. There's an extra joke and an
extra punch line that don't go together and won't be used.

A. A TURKEY LAUGHING ITS HEAD OFF.

B. IS TURKEY SOUP GOOD
FOR YOUR HEALTH?

C. DRUMSTICKS.

D. WHAT GOES "GOBBLE,
GOBBLE, HA-HA, PLOP"?

E. HE WAS STUFFED.

F. WHY DID THE TURKEY
CROSS THE ROAD?

G. NOT IF YOU'RE A TURKEY.

H. WHY DIDN'T THE TURKEY
EAT ANYTHING?

TV Flops

**Uncle John loves stuff that's so bad it's . . .
well . . . funny! Like these four failed TV shows.**

Cop Rock

What it was: Imagine a combination of *CSI* and *Glee*.
Airing on ABC in 1990, *Cop Rock* looked like any
other gritty police drama. And then . . . the officers
started singing and dancing. Millions of viewers tuned
in to the first show out of curiosity (singing cops?).
They were also interested because the series was
created by Steven Bochco. His 1980s police drama,
Hill Street Blues, had been a big hit.
Cancelled! Viewers laughed at *Cop Rock*. But it
wasn't supposed to be a comedy. Critics called it "one
of the worst TV shows ever." It lasted 11 episodes
before ABC locked it up and threw away the key.

My Mother the Car

What it was: This 1965 NBC sitcom was about a
man who buys a car that is possessed by the spirit of
his dead mother. Mom's ghost talks to him through
the car's radio.
Cancelled! With low ratings and horrible reviews, the
show ran out of gas after just one season. One good
thing came out it: James L. Brooks's first TV writing
job was an episode of *My Mother the Car*. Two
decades later, he co-created *The Simpsons*.

Cavemen

What it was: Three prehistoric cavemen must adapt to modern life in 2007. The idea promised a lot of laughs. And viewers were already familiar with the main characters. They'd been featured in Geico auto insurance commercials. Nine million eager viewers tuned in to the first episode.

Cancelled! Fewer than half of those viewers tuned in to the second episode. ABC cancelled the show after six. Why? *Cavemen* was what critics call a "one-joke premise." In each show, three bearded men with big foreheads try to find their way in the modern world. But they can't, so they whine and grunt a lot. It got old fast.

Homeboys in Outer Space

What it was: This 1996 show followed two street-talkin' space cadets (Morris and Ty) who fly around the universe in their winged low-rider car, the *Space Hoopty*. They were guided by their sassy female space computer, Loquatia (lo-KWAY-sha).

Cancelled! *Homeboys* had a lot of famous guest stars, such as James Doohan who played Scotty on the original *Star Trek* series. The show was meant to spoof sci-fi blockbusters. In an episode called "Return of the Jed Eye," a space bounty hunter named Jed Eye hijacks the Hoopty. Sound funny? Well . . . one critic said the show was "so offensive it makes you cringe instead of laugh."

How Low to Go

In these sports, the lowest score wins.

Golf

The object of the game is to get the ball into the hole with as few shots as possible. So, a score of 4 is better than a score of 5. Most golf courses are either 9 holes or 18. Scores are added for the full course.

Cross-Country Running

The first five finishers on a cross-country team score the points. The race winner scores 1 point, second place scores 2, and so on. A perfect score for a team is 15 points. (Add 1, 2, 3, 4, and 5 to see why).

Body-Building

In body-building, men and women are judged on the size and symmetry of their muscles. Judges rank the athletes, with the lowest score for the competitor judged to be the best. All of the judges' scores are added together, and the lowest total is the winner.

And Then There's . . .

Limbo! In a limbo competition, going lower is the goal. Dancers bend backward to pass under a long skinny stick without touching it. The stick is lowered for each round. The winner is the last to limbo without touching or falling. (*Limbo* is a variation of the word *limber*.)

Dino-Score

Hold the book so this page lies flat, as shown. Sit up straight and hold a hand behind your head with your pinky finger sticking out. Close your eyes, bring your hand over your head and down to this page. What did your pinky land on? Mark down the score and repeat five times.

Answer on page 284

139

Ghostly Snapshots

Our sources say that if you follow these guidelines, you'll have a 90 percent chance of taking a picture of a ghost, whether you believe in spooks . . . or not!

1. Pick a Location

Graveyards, battlefields, and old hotels are all thought to be ripe with spirits. "These special places may be ports into the next dimension," says Dr. Oester, head of the International Ghost Hunters Society (IGHS). But you don't have to leave home to take ghost photos. Boston ghost hunter Kriss Stephens says ghosts like to hang out in basements, attics, and . . . bathrooms.

2. Watch the Weather

Avoid shooting outdoors during rainy, misty, or foggy weather. Ghosts, according to the IGHS, often appear as glowing orbs—circles of light—in photos. But drops of water look like orbs in photos, too. If you decide to hunt for ghosts in the bathroom, don't shoot into mirrors (or toilets). The camera's flash can bounce off reflective surfaces and cause ghostly shapes to show up in photos.

3. Wait until Dark

Stephens says ghosts seem to prefer the dark. Be sure to point the camera away from streetlights, metal signs, the moon, and fireflies. Any light source or reflective surface can create "fake" ghost photos.

4. Never Ghost Hunt Alone

"It is easier to investigate an old dark cemetery if other people are with you," Dr. Oester says. Be sure to obey all posted signs. Who knows what a ghost (or the night watchman or—even worse—your parents) might do if you ignore the "Closed at Dusk" sign?

5. Bring the Right Equipment

Most ghost hunters think digital cameras work best for capturing ghostly pictures. Be sure the camera has a built-in flash. Always take at least two shots, without moving a muscle . . . except your fingertip. *Click!*

6. Don't Spook the Spooks

Walk around for a while to let the ghosts get used to your presence. And be sure to speak softly so you don't scare them away.

7. Point, Aim, Click!

Take photos of people. "Ghosts like to hang out with the living," says Stephens. And, she says, they like to follow the living, too. So take some shots of what's behind you. Ghosts also like to hang around in doorways and gates. Don't be surprised if one of them is waiting to show you the exit when you leave.

How to Defrost a Woolly Mammoth

Here's how scientists melted away a whole lot of ice to reveal a 20,000-year-old behemoth.

Mammoth-sicle

When nine-year-old reindeer herder Simion Jarkov spotted a giant curved tusk sticking out of the snow, he knew it was valuable. What he didn't know: the tusk was still attached to the frozen body of an 11-foot-tall woolly mammoth. The mammoth had been preserved for centuries in the remote Siberian wilderness. Two years later, in 1999, an international team of experts including French mammoth hunter Bernard Buigues and Dutch paleontologist Dick Mol took on the challenge of digging the behemoth out of the permafrost.

Dig That Woolly Beast

The Siberian permafrost consists of layers of ice, frozen mud, and clay. In the area where the mammoth was found, the permafrost has not thawed since it formed, 11,000 years ago at the end of the last ice age. Buigues and his team used jackhammers to dig down through the frozen ground. They dug a trench all the way around the mammoth. And then they chiseled beneath it. They ended up with a 26-ton block of mammoth and frozen earth, with two huge tusks sticking out. After securing the block in a harness, they transported it 150 miles away, dangling beneath a helicopter.

"This is a first," said Larry Agenbroad, another team member. "It's the first time that a Pleistocene animal as big as a mammoth has been brought up still encased in its tomb of permafrost and airlifted to where it could be studied."

Does My Fur Look OK?

The chopper and its rare cargo set down next to an ice cave carved out near the city of Khatanga, Siberia. The iced mammoth was carefully wedged into the cave. And the slow process of revealing its secrets began.

The mammoth's temperature was 11 degrees Fahrenheit, still far below freezing. The problem: When an animal has been dead for thousands of years, if it defrosts quickly, it will begin to rot. Buigues wanted to thaw the mammoth slowly and try to keep its flesh, well, fresh.

He found a solution: blow dryers, the kind used for styling hair. Working in 30-minute time periods, the scientists began to slowly warm up the mammoth.

Still Green after All These Years

As the mammoth and the chunk of earth around it began to thaw, the scientists discovered green plants surrounding the animal's body. Buigues ran his hands through a patch of the mammoth's thick reddish-brown hair. "It was like touching a live animal," he said.

And . . . like smelling one. The mammoth wasn't the only thing frozen in the block of ice. Its poop was frozen in there with it. "It was like walking into the stall at the zoo where the elephants sleep," said Mol. "Suddenly you could smell dung and urine."

By keeping the mammoth flesh fresh, Buigues hoped to recover DNA that could be used for something that sounds almost like science fiction: cloning an extinct animal. "Most paleontologists don't believe it's possible," Buigues admits, "but science moves fast."

Clone Sweet Clone

Especially in Japan. Akira Iritani, a professor at Japan's Kyoto University, tried several times to use skin and muscle cells from the Siberian mammoth for cloning. It didn't work. The cells had been damaged by frost.

Now Iritani has a new method that allows him to extract DNA from frozen—instead of thawed—cells. He claims that by 2016, he will have cloned a mammoth embryo (fertilized egg) and implanted it into a female African elephant. About 600 days later, he hopes to see the birth of the first baby woolly mammoth since prehistoric times.

Remember

Try to memorize this list of 12 words and repeat it without looking. Most people have trouble doing that. Did you?

Word list

MOUSE
PENCIL
RED
SNAKE
HOOP
ARROW
APPLE
IDEA
SUN
CAT
JUMP
FEATHER

But here's a trick that'll give you a much better chance. Just create a wacky picture in your mind using the words in order.

For example, below is a picture we thought up for those 12 words: a mouse holding a pencil, with a red snake around it, and so on.

BUT you don't need to draw anything— just imagine it in your mind!

Now try memorizing the list again, this time creating a mental picture. Any better?

Earth's Shadow

The Moon isn't the only thing following Earth around the Sun. Turns out we have a tagalong!

Stop Following Me!

Asteroids are small, rocky pieces of space rubble. Scientists estimate there are millions of them in our solar system. Most are in the region between Mars and Jupiter. Astronomers disagree on how they ended up there. Some think they're part of a planet that was blown apart. Others think they're rocks that never formed into a planet in the first place. Either way, there's one asteroid that—for some reason—is following our planet in its orbit around the Sun.

Me and My Shadow

Earth's little shadow has a boring name: 2010 SO16. But scientists are excited about the mystery it presents. Did it come from the asteroid belt between Mars and Jupiter? Did it break off of our moon long ago? Or is it left over from when our planet formed, 4.5 billion years ago?

Wherever the chunk of rock came from, it never gets closer to us than about 10 million miles. "It keeps well away from Earth," says astronomer Tolis Christou, who studies the asteroid. "So well, in fact, that it has likely been in this orbit for several hundred thousand years."

Back Off!

Most near-Earth asteroids (NEAs) have egg-shaped orbits that take them through the inner solar system. Not 2010 SO16. Its orbit is almost circular, like Earth's . . . but with a really strange twist.

As the asteroid comes toward Earth, the planet's gravity pushes it into a larger orbit that takes longer to go around the Sun. As Earth catches up with the asteroid, the planet's gravity pushes it into a smaller orbit that takes it closer to the Sun. This slingshot effect makes the asteroid's orbit look like a round horseshoe with the Earth in the opening between the two ends. It takes the asteroid 175 years to get from one end of the horseshoe to the other.

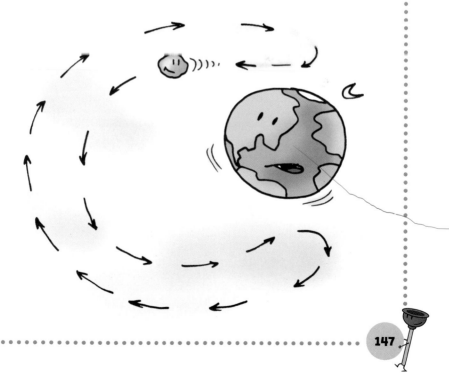

Out of This World

Amaze your friends with these asteroid facts.

Small Worlds. Most asteroids are tiny (like grains of sand), but some are a few miles across. Ceres, by far the biggest, is about 590 miles wide, about the same width as the state of Montana.

What Is That Thing? Ceres was the first asteroid discovered (its size helped). It was spotted on January 1, 1801, by Italian astronomer Giuseppe Piazzi. At first he thought the asteroid was a star. Then he thought it might be a comet or the "missing planet" astronomers of the time thought had once been between Jupiter and Mars. The term "asteroid" (which means "starlike") wasn't used until 1802.

Brrr! The average temperature on an asteroid is -100 degrees Fahrenheit.

No Swimming. Scientists have found evidence that at least two asteroids have water. (It's frozen, of course.)

Tiny Moons. Some asteroids have their own satellites, or moons. Asteroid 1994 CC has two moons. They're each about as wide as half a football field.

That's All? Even though there are millions of asteroids in our solar system, if you crunched them all into a single ball, it would be smaller than our moon.

Watch Out!

In case a huge asteroid heads our way, scientists are figuring out how to prevent a disaster.

Send Bruce Willis! That's what happens in the movie *Armageddon*. Willis leads a team of oil rig workers determined to blow up an asteroid and save Earth. Bad idea: Scientists say blowing up an asteroid would cause *lots* of rocks to smash into our planet. It's best to try to change its path so it won't hit Earth.

Light It Up! Spacecraft carrying giant mirrors point the Sun's rays at the asteroid's surface. Vaporized rock shoots into space and alters the asteroid's path.

Space Smash! Crash a spacecraft into the asteroid. A mangled spacecraft might add enough weight to the rock to change its path.

Laser Attack! Set up lasers on the Moon and shoot the asteroid. Hit it enough times and you'll cause an explosion. The asteroid won't break apart, but it might change course.

Blast It! Set off a large nuclear explosion near an asteroid. That might be enough to change its path.

Asteroids do come close to Earth, so scientists keep an eye on them. They say no huge asteroids are due in our neighborhood for the next 100 years. (Note to scientists: Bruce Willis won't be around by then, so keep the ideas coming!)

Answers on
page 278

What's What?

What do these words and phrases mean?
Figuring them out might require both thinking and guessing.
Write the numbers in the blanks and see how you do.

1. DISME

2. DRAGEES

3. DUST JACKET

4. ERUCTATION

5. GLABELLA

6. PAINTED LADY

7. PLEWDS

8. WIDOW'S PEAK

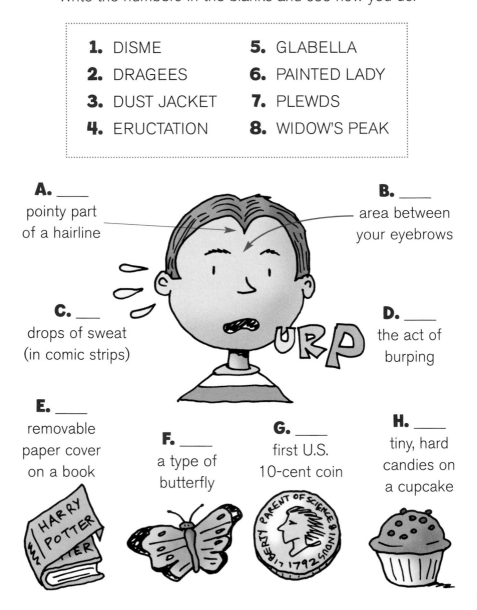

A. ____
pointy part
of a hairline

B. ____
area between
your eyebrows

C. ____
drops of sweat
(in comic strips)

D. ____
the act of
burping

E. ____
removable
paper cover
on a book

F. ____
a type of
butterfly

G. ____
first U.S.
10-cent coin

H. ____
tiny, hard
candies on
a cupcake

Brain Farts

Ever have a brain fart? Uncle John has.
And so did the students who wrote these answers
on tests. See how many mistakes you can find.

1. On April 14, 1865, Lincoln went to the theater and got shot in his seat by one of the actors.

2. Under the Constitution the people enjoyed the right to keep bare arms.

3. The King wore a scarlet robe trimmed with vermin.

4. *Magnet:* Something you find crawling all over a dead cat.

5. One of the causes of the Revolutionary War was the English put tacks in their tea.

6. Queen Victoria sat on a thorn for 63 years.

7. To collect fumes of sulfur, hold a deacon over a flame in a test tube.

8. *Equator:* An imaginary lion running around the Earth through Africa.

9. The pistol of a flower is its only protection against insects.

10. Finally the colonists won the War and no longer had to pay for taxis.

Answers on pages 278-279

Dirty Jobs

Let's face it: History was filthy. And these
examples of jobs from the past prove it.

De-Lousiest Job

In the Middle Ages, bugs were everywhere, especially
in people's hair. It was not polite to scratch or to pick
bugs off in public, so wealthy people hired someone
else to do it. Clients sat in the sun while professional
nitpickers plucked nits (louse eggs), lice, and fleas
from their hair.

Chairmen of Muck

In the 1700s, London's muddy streets were covered
with piles of trash and heaps of manure. It was gross.
Well-dressed ladies and gentlemen refused to walk in
the muck. So they hired men to carry them in sedan
chairs. Sedan chairs looked a bit like telephone
booths sitting on top of two sturdy poles. Two chair
men lifted the sedan and carried it through the
streets, one man in front and one in back. The man in
the back had the worst job. He couldn't see what the
guy in front jumped over, so . . . he stepped in it.

Poop Scooper

In the early 1800s, leather tanners soaked animal
hides in stinky solutions. One of these mixtures was
made from water and dog poop. At the time, there

were no plastic bags, pooper-scoopers, or rubber gloves. Tanners paid kids to collect poop from the streets. The kids walked around the city, picked up dog poop with their bare hands and put it into buckets to carry back to the tanner. Their pay? A shilling per bucket—equal to about 12 pennies.

More Dirty Jobs . . .

And why you wouldn't want them.

Woad Dyers used the woad plant to dye wool blue. They ended up with blue hands, and they smelled like rotting boiled cabbage mixed with sewage.

Toshers picked through the sludge in London's sewers. If they were lucky, they found treasure: a few coins or pieces of jewelry that had been dropped on the street and had washed through the drains into the muck. Biggest drawback? The rats.

Breaker Boys worked for 10 hours a day picking slate out of coal on a moving conveyor belt. If a finger, hand, or arm got caught in the moving belt? It could be sliced right off.

Gooseherds spent their days walking and their nights watching for foxes as they herded geese into town. Sometimes they trudged for a hundred miles just to deliver a single goose for a Christmas feast.

Tooth Donors let dentists pull their teeth and transplant them into someone else's mouth.

Ogre Drool

Can you find the one path from this slobbery ogre to the mop?

start

155

Answer on page 284

Answers on
page 279

Ship Shape

Number these 10 pictures to show in
what order this model was put together.

A. ____

B. ____

C. ____

D. ____
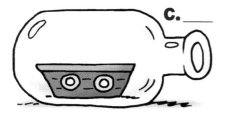

E. ____

F. ____

G. ____

H. ____

I. ____
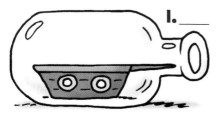

J. ____

Crazy Crazes

Get out your pencil and fill in the blanks in this quiz. RULES: You can only use letters from the phrase THOSE MAD CRAZES WILL NEVER STOP.

1. In 1992 the Video Phone flopped. No one wanted to pay $1,500 for a phone that would let them see their friends with bed __ __ A __ .

2. The poster for the first movie in Smell-O-Vision said, "First they moved! Then they talked! Now they __ M __ __ L ."

3. In the 1960s, American kids went crazy for wild-haired, naked, pot-bellied dolls called T __ __ __ L __ .

4. A Swedish doctor created a way for people to lose weight: Eat like a __ __ V __ M __ __ .

5. Bit Critter, Digital Doggie, and Micro Chimp were all part of the virtual __ __ T craze that started in 1997.

6. Back in 1957, you could put your money in a pie-o-matic vending machine. What came out? __ __ Z Z __ .

7. The goopy stuff that went up and down in those lava L___ P popular in the 1960s was made from carbon tetrachloride and wax.

8. Girls danced the frug wearing __ __ P __ __ dresses, but they didn't go out in the rain!

9. Before email, kids had __ __ N pals.

Answers on page 279

The Talking Seal

Think it's tough to teach a parrot to talk?
Imagine trying to teach a seal!

Harboring Hoover

In 1971, fisherman George Swallow and his wife, Alice, adopted an orphaned Atlantic harbor seal pup. The baby seal slurped up fish so fast they named him after a vacuum cleaner brand: "Hoover." What they didn't know was that Hoover would grow up to be a star at Boston's New England Aquarium.

Hard Story to Swallow

As a baby, Hoover lived in the bathtub at the Swallow's house. He was treated like a member of the family, even going for rides in the car. When Hoover got too big for the family tub, he was moved to the pond behind the house. Before long, Hoover needed more room (and fish) than the Swallows could give him. They took him to the New England Aquarium and told the keepers that Hoover was no ordinary seal—he could talk. At first, the keepers found the Swallows' story hard to believe. That soon changed.

Ah'm Tawkin'

Visitors to the aquarium were used to talking parrots, but a talking harbor seal? "Get outta here!" Hoover barked when visitors came near his tank. He also said "Hello there!" and "How are ya?" And he could even say his name. Hoover spoke with a heavy Boston accent, so he didn't pronounce "r" sounds.

**"Ah final ahs disappeah.
Wheah they go, we've no idear."**

When he said "there," it sounded like "they-ah." "Are" sounded like "ah." And when he bellowed out his name, it sounded like "Hoo-vah." He picked up the accent from the Swallows, just like kids pick up their parents' accents when they learn to talk. And he learned to "talk" all by himself. The Swallows never tried to teach him!

Even in Noo Yawk

There have been stories in the past of dogs, cats, and even an elephant that could mimic human language. But keepers at the New England Aquarium claim that Hoover was the first nonhuman mammal to produce the kinds of sounds he made.

As his fame spread, Hoover was featured on the television show *Good Morning America*. Stories about the talking seal appeared in magazines such as *Reader's Digest* and *The New Yorker*. Hoover was so well-known that when he died of old age in 1981, he got his own obituary in the *Boston Globe*. "For 13 years, Hoover was our goodwill ambassador to the world," said an aquarium spokesman. "Visitors will surely miss his cheerful 'hello there.'"

Tawkin' Bawstin

Bostonians don't just drop the *r* in their words. They make up words for everyday things. See if you can match each word with its meaning.

1. ___ Cabbage Night
2. ___ American chop suey
3. ___ Bobos
4. ___ Gahkablahka
5. ___ Spuckie

6. ___ B'daydahs
7. ___ Tonic
8. ___ Wiffle
9. ___ Banger
10. ___ Potty platta

A. Macaroni with hamburger, tomato sauce, and a bit of onion and green pepper.

B. Potatoes served mashed, boiled, or fried.

C. The night before Halloween, a time for throwing things such as cabbages and eggs.

D. A platter of deli food you get for a party.

E. A traffic tie-up caused by people looking at an accident.

F. Boat shoes (which is what Bostonians call Keds).

G. A really bad headache.

H. A crew-cut done with electric clippers.

I. A hero sandwich named for spucadella, a type of Italian sandwich roll.

J. Soda pop.

Answers on page 279

Answers on page 279

Moon Code

A new restaurant has opened up on the moon.
Its specialties are moon pies and green cheese.
Use the KEY to see how the restaurant was reviewed.

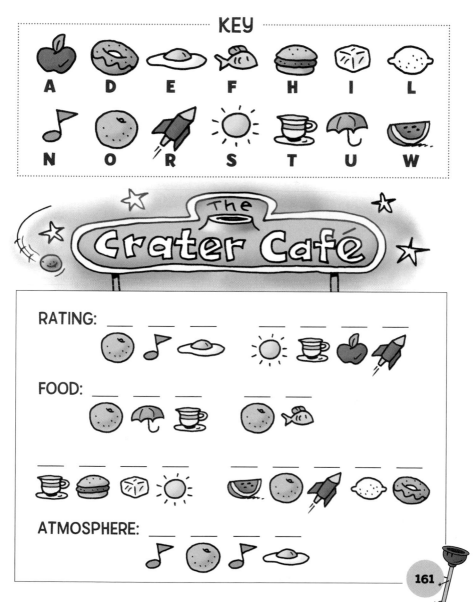

KEY

A D E F H I L

N O R S T U W

The Crater Café

RATING: ___ ___ ___   ___ ___ ___ ___

FOOD: ___ ___ ___   ___ ___

___ ___ ___ ___   ___ ___ ___ ___ ___

ATMOSPHERE: ___ ___ ___ ___

Nüshu!

*Here's a story about a language that was
kept secret for hundreds of years . . . from men.*

No Girls Allowed

In Chinese, the words *nü shu* mean "women's writing."
And that's just what Nüshu is. Pronounced *noo shoo*,
it's a written language that was created hundreds of
years ago by women, for women. They used it to
secretly communicate with each other. Why? Because
Chinese girls and women were not allowed to read or
write Chinese. They could only speak it. After the
young women got married, they were rarely allowed
to leave their homes. There was no way for them to
write letters to their friends. (This was long before
phones were invented.)

So the women who lived in a remote part of Hunan
Province in southern China decided to create the
Nüshu language. Mothers passed it down to their
daughters. And when those girls grew up, they
passed it down to *their* daughters. They wrote down
their hopes and dreams in secret diaries. They even
printed secret Nüshu messages on quilts, fans, and
other artwork.

Hidden in Plain Sight

How did the girls keep their language a secret? They
made sure that it looked like gibberish to men. In

Nüshu, each written character represents a sound. (That's how English letters work, too.) But the Chinese language that was used by men is different: The characters each represent an entire word. Men who happened to see the written Nüshu language didn't know it was a language at all! They thought it was a lot of pretty symbols with no meaning.

The Secret Is Out

The Nüshu language was hidden so well that historians are not even sure when it began. They believe it is at least 400 years old and maybe more than 1,000 years old. And for most of that time, men had no clue that Nüshu existed. When the Chinese government learned about it in the 1960s, they thought it was a secret code used by spies!

Today, the Nüshu language is almost gone. That's because girls don't need it anymore. Now, girls are taught to read and write, along with the boys. There are very few women left who can read Nüshu. One of them was Yang Huanyi, who died in 2004 when she was 98 years old. "When I was little," she said, "we girls used to get together and sing and talk, and that's when we learned Nüshu from one another. It made our lives better because we could express ourselves that way."

Language experts are trying to learn everything they can about Nüshu. That way, they can preserve it before it goes away forever.

The Legend of the Goat Sucker

Is this terrifying creature real?
Or is it just a legend?

Jeepers Creepers

Some say the legend began in March, 1975, near a small Puerto Rican town called Moca. Local papers reported animal killings: Birds, horses, and goats had been found dead, drained of blood. All of the animals had deep puncture wounds on their bodies.

At first, people called the killer *El Vampiro de Moca* (The Vampire of Moca). Then the sightings spread to Mexico, Latin America, and even the United States. Because the creatures were mostly reported by Spanish-speaking people, some began to call it "the Hispanic vampire."

The beast most people said they saw was bipedal (two-legged). It was hairless, with large red eyes, deadly fangs, and rows of sharp spikes sticking out of its spine. It often feasted on sheep and goats. So as tales spread, the creature's name changed to *Los Chupacabras*. (In Spanish, chupar means "to suck" and cabra means "goat.")

The Real Culprit

Here's the problem: Eyewitnesses say they've seen chupacabras. But there is no proof. Video clips of the "goat sucker" show hairless four-legged animals, not the two-legged beasts from the legends. Scientists think the videos show diseased canine breeds, such as foxes or coyotes, that have lost all their hair. And a mite, not a monster, is to blame.

Barry O'Connor, a biologist from the University of Michican, says that an eight-legged mite called *Sarcoptes scabiei* is the true bloodsucker. The mite burrows under the skin of coyotes and other canines. Mites are parasites: They live off their hosts' bodies. They clog an animal's hair follicles and cause its fur to fall out. Itchy, damaged skin can become infected, which can lead to the animal's death. O'Connor says that large numbers of burrowing mites can cause "chupacabras syndrome." Infected canines turn into "naked, leathery, smelly monstrosities."

Where'd You Get That Mite?

Animals get this vicious blood-sucker from . . . humans. In people, *Sarcoptes scabiei* causes an itchy rash known as scabies. The mites spread from people to their pet dogs. Then they hop from pet dogs onto wild canines, such as foxes, wolves, and coyotes.

As for diseased canines killing goats, O'Connor says it could happen. "These animals are greatly weakened. They're going to have a hard time hunting." While the mites are sucking on their canine hosts, the hosts feed on livestock—such as sheep and, of course, goats. And that feeds the legend.

Answers on
page 279

A Filling Joke

Fill in the name of each item below. When you're done, place
each of those words in the boxes on the next page so that the
yellow squares match up. There's only one way they'll all fit.

Finally, read DOWN the yellow column to find the joke's answer.

G H O S T

Why did the monster eat only the candles on his birthday cake?

G H O S T

Uncle John's Stall of Fame

We're always amazed by the fun things that people make out of toilets and toilet paper.

Bathroom Heroes: Dave Hersch and his 10-year-old son, Miles
What They Did: They made a car...out of two toilets.
True Story: The Hersches wanted to ride around their Colorado neighborhood in style. So Dave removed the seat from a go-kart and replaced it with an actual toilet. But he didn't bolt it down. When Dave made his first turn, the toilet slid off onto the street. "It broke into a million pieces," he said. The Hersches didn't give up. They built a better, safer toilet car. Now, it has two toilets to sit on. Also, there are six holders for toilet-paper rolls, a magazine rack for bathroom reading (woo hoo!), and a cooler for snacks. Dave and Miles say that their toilet car is a great way for them to get to know their neighbors.

Bathroom Heroes: A team of Chinese artists
What They Did: They constructed a new "Great Wall of China" out of...you guessed it...toilets.
True Story: The 2009 "Festival of Ceramics" in China was all about creating interesting art out of ceramic materials. Well, it just so happens that toilets and sinks are made of ceramics. So the team of artists

gathered thousands of old toilets and sinks (and cleaned them, we hope). Then they stacked them in rows, with the bowls facing out, to form a massive wall. The wall is more than 300 feet long, and stands nearly 20 feet tall. The artists added plumbing and turned on the water to create the Great Toilet Waterfall.

Bathroom Hero: Susan Brennan, a young woman from Michigan

What She Did: She made a wedding dress out of toilet paper, and won $1,000!

True Story: Susan is a former high-school cheerleader who wants to become a fashion designer. She's off to a great start. In 2011 she entered the 7th annual "Toilet Paper Wedding Dress Contest." It's hosted by a website called cheap-chic-weddings.com. They received more than 800 entries that year, and Susan's was the best. How'd she make the winning dress? "I used tape and glue," said Susan. "A *lot* of tape and glue." And a lot of toilet paper, too. Susan even used toilet paper to make feathers and flowers. The wedding dress looks so much like the real thing, it's hard to believe it was made out of TP!

On a diet?

No, I was used for a wedding dress!

Plug Your Nose!

A warning from Uncle John: Brain-eating creatures may be lurking in your favorite swimming hole. Here's how to fight them.

Stirring Up Trouble

Each summer, as temperatures rise, water in ponds, lakes, creeks, and rivers begins to evaporate. And a single-celled amoeba called *Naegleria fowleri* stirs from the murky depths.

Enter an unsuspecting swimmer—you. It's hot and you can't wait to cool down. So you dive into the water headfirst. Your hands touch the muddy bottom and stir up the muck—and the creatures lurking there. Single-celled amoebas swirl into the water and flood your nostrils.

Within seven days, the amoebas have traveled from your nose to your brain. But you don't know it. You feel feverish. You can't keep food down. You have a headache and a stiff neck. It's not the flu: It's *Naegleria fowleri*, eating your brain cells.

Beating the Odds

In 98 percent of known cases, within a few days of infection, victims of the brain-eating amoebas die. Pretty scary, right? Worse yet, there is no known cure. But take heart. Infection by *Naegleria fowleri* is rare. Most years, not a single case is reported to the Center for Disease Control in Atlanta, Georgia—the organization created to track all U.S. medical events. Some years, two or three people fall victim to infection. But that's on the entire North American continent. You're more likely to be struck by lightning than to sniff up these tiny water-born killers.

A Pinch of Prevention

Still don't like the odds? Wear nose plugs when you jump into those swimming holes. If amoebas can't get into your nose, they can't eat your brain. Better yet, stick to chlorinated swimming pools. *Naegleria fowleri* can't survive in chemically-purified water.

Brain Jigglers

Laugh, and your brain laughs with you.

Q: What kind of fish can do brain surgery?
A: A neurosturgeon.

Q: What do you call an empty skull?
A: A no-brainer.

Q: When did Benjamin Franklin discover electricity?
A: During a brainstorm.

Q: What do you call a jail for smart people?
A: A brain cell.

Q: Why did Einstein go to the beach?
A: To catch a brainwave.

Q: What word do brainy kids always spell wrong?
A: Wrong.

The Microbe

Here's a poem about a tiny subject by French writer and historian Hilaire Belloc (1870–1953).

The Microbe is so very small

You cannot make him out at all,

But many sanguine people hope

To see him through a microscope.

His jointed tongue that lies beneath

A hundred curious rows of teeth;

His seven tufted tails with lots

Of lovely pink and purple spots,

On each of which a pattern stands,

Composed of forty separate bands;

His eyebrows of a tender green;

All these have never yet been seen—

But Scientists, who ought to know,

Assure us that they must be so . . . .

Oh! let us never, never doubt

What nobody is sure about!

Fake Phlegm

Feel a sneeze coming on? Get your tissue ready!

What You Need:

- Small bowl
- 3–4 tablespoons cornstarch
- 2 tablespoons water
- Green food coloring
- Spoon
- Tissue

Preparation:

1. Put the cornstarch and water in the bowl. Add a single drop of green food coloring. Stir the mixture together until the green is blended in and all of the powdery cornstarch has dissolved in the water.

2. If the mixture seems too wet, add a little more cornstarch. If it's too dry, sprinkle in more water.

The Prank: Spoon a glob of the goo onto a tissue. Sneak up behind your victim. Let your best fake sneeze rip, and then dangle the tissue as close to the person as you can. (Extra points for grossing out adults!)

One Way

What a mess of one-way roads!
Following the arrows, find a
way to the amusement park.
Good luck!

Winnie's Fun Land

End

Answer on page 285

Classic 'Bots

Not all television stars are flesh and blood.

Robby the Robot

- Robby the Robot was "born" in 1955, weighing in at 300 pounds and standing 7'1" tall. He looked a bit like a pot-belly stove with a clear dome for a head and giant pincers for hands.

- Robby was built for the 1956 science-fiction blockbuster *Forbidden Planet* and cost $125,000.

- He guest-starred in many television series, including *The Twilight Zone*, *Gilligan's Island*, *Mork and Mindy*, and *The Addams Family*. He joined his "brother," B-9, in two episodes of *Lost in Space*.

- In 1981, Robby the Robot played the part of "Squeezak" in a Charmin toilet-paper commercial. His big line? "Don't squeeze the Charmin!"

- A full-size Robby the Robot replica can be purchased for about $30,000—shipping included!

B-9

- Can robots have family? Robby does. He has a "little brother" named B-9 (nicknamed "Blinky").

- B-9 starred in the series *Lost in Space* from 1965 to 1969. A Hollywood announcer named Dick Tufeld was the voice of B-9. On the TV show, B-9 went by the name "Robot" or "The Robot." And his most famous phrase was "Danger, Will Robinson!"

• There were actually two different versions of B-9. A prop suit was worn by actor Bill May for close-ups, and a stunt robot was used for distant shots.

• The original B-9 stunt robot is in storage in the Science Fiction Museum and Hall of Fame in Seattle, Washington. But anyone who wants to buy an exact replica can. The price? $24,500.

Twiki

• Twiki (TWEE-kee) co-starred in the series *Buck Rogers in the 25th Century* from 1979 to 1981. The name comes from the model number: TWKE-4.

• Twiki was a kid-sized silver robot. In the series, the role of Twiki was played by 3'11" tall Italian actor Felix Anthony Silla. (Silla also played "Cousin Itt" on *The Addams Family*.)

• Twiki's voice, including his trademark phrase ("bidi-bidi-bidi") may sound familiar. Mel Blanc, the voice of Daffy Duck and Bugs Bunny was the voice actor.

• Twiki used that phrase to express his love in the episode "Cruise Ship to the Stars." The object of his affection? A girl robot named Tina. She answered him with "boodi-boodi-boodi."

Plumbing Pioneers

Two inventions that made water safer.

Inventor: Al Moen, a college student from Seattle, Washington

Invention: The single-handle faucet

Story: One day in 1937, Al was washing his hands when a burst of scalding water burned his skin. That was a common problem at the time. Sinks had two handles—one for hot water, the other for cold. And they didn't always work right. "I thought about it," Al said. "And I knew a single-handle faucet was the answer. So I began to make some drawings." It took Al five years to perfect his design—a faucet with one handle that controls both hot *and* cold water. He also improved the design of two-handled faucets. Al made it easier to control water temperature, and people stopped getting burned . . . most of the time.

Inventor: Luther Haws, a plumber from Berkeley, California

Invention: The drinking fountain

Story: In 1906 Luther saw some school kids drinking water out of a tin cup that was chained to a sink. Luther knew that sharing a cup could spread germs and diseases, so he had an idea. Using old plumbing parts, he invented the modern drinking fountain. Today's water fountains use the same basic design that Luther invented more than a century ago.

Altered Art

*Here's how to turn a thrift-store painting
into a comical or terrifying masterpiece.*

What You Need:

- Thrift-store painting
- Acrylic paints
- Paintbrushes
- Newspaper

Preparation:

1. Set your paints and brushes out on some old newspaper sheets.

2. Put your thrift-store painting in the center of the paper, and think about how to add some fun. Does the painting have bushes? You could paint *T. rex* or a pirate peeking out from behind them. If the painting has a ship at sea, you could paint a giant squid trying to drag it down or flying saucers attacking from above. If the painting shows a cityscape, add a giant Barbie doll towering above a city skyline or a robot parade in the street. The sillier (or scarier) the better!

3. When you've decided on the best idea, paint it.

4. Let your artwork dry overnight, and then have a parent help you hang it on the wall.

Take the Stinky Pee Test

On page 120 we told you about the asparagus pee gene. Some kids have it. Some don't. Are you brave enough to take the test?

What You Need:

- 1 bunch fresh asparagus
- Olive oil
- Salt
- Parmesan cheese
- Baking sheet
- Your nose

Preparation:

1. Preheat the oven to 450 degrees. Wash the asparagus spears and trim off the tough ends.

2. Place spears on baking sheet. Drizzle olive oil over them. Sprinkle on salt and Parmesan cheese.

3. Roast for about 10 minutes. Then eat it up.

The Test: The next time you need to pee, do the sniff test. Just inhale through your nose. If your pee smells like rotten eggs, then you have the "asparagus pee gene." If it doesn't, you don't.

Bonus: Talk your whole family into taking the test. Your genes come from your parents. So if you have the gene, at least one of them will, too!

Stick 'em Up!

Here's a good way to have some fun with a pen and a pad of self-adhesive notes. Use our suggestions or come up with your own messages—then stick 'em up!

100%
BAD
NEWS

on a bathroom mirror

next to a sink

DAMP
WHEN
WET

FREE:
TAKE ONE

above a toilet paper roll

DON'T
READ
THIS!

anywhere

the front door →

GO
AWAY

THIS IS
MY BEST
SIDE

on someone's back

DRY
PAINT

I May Be
Late, but
I'm Ahead
of You

on a painted surface

What's Cooking?

Victorian naturalist Frank Buckland lived,
breathed, and . . . ate the animals he studied.

End World Hunger

In the late 1800s, Dr. Frank Buckland caused quite a stir in England. Like some other scientists, he thought a time might come when there would be too many people in Britain. The country's farms would not be able to feed them all. So Dr. Buckland set up a society to find tasty new foods. On the menu: silkworms, beavers, parrots, and other unusual items.

Mice Taste Nice

Frank Buckland got his weird tastes from his father, William Buckland, who spent his life studying animals. The senior Buckland claimed to have eaten through the entire animal kingdom, all in the name of science.

Thanks to his dad, young Frank learned how scientists work: They ask questions, such as "Are mice tasty?" To answer that question, they would collect data (mice), do experiments (cook the mice), and analyze the data (eat the mice).

A lot of testing happened at the Buckland breakfast table. Frank's dad invited some of the leading scientists of his day to try out new recipes. Mice on buttered toast was a hit. Hedgehog was "good and tender," but crocodile . . . that was a disaster. None of his guests could gulp it down.

Even bugs made it onto the menu. Frank thought fried earwigs tasted "horribly bitter." His father said nothing tasted more terrible than fat bluebottle flies.

Deathly Dinners

After Frank grew up, he became a doctor. He often treated sick animals at the London Zoo. Sometimes he could not save his patients, so . . . he ate them. That's how Elephant Trunk Soup, Panther Chops, and Rhinoceros Pie ended up on his dinner table. After a fire at the zoo, Dr. Buckland served "Accidentally Roasted Giraffe" to dinner guests.

Dr. Buckland's methods may seem mad, but his goal was to do good. He was willing to taste-test every bug or beast that came his way, if it would help to keep England's people from starving.

We'd Rather Starve

On July 12, 1862, Frank Buckland's society held its first official dinner. The menu included Bird's Nest Soup, Sea Slug Soup, and Deer Sinew Soup. Buckland thought the soups all tasted like glue. The Kangaroo Stew was "not bad, but a little gone off."

Dr. Buckland's exotic meals didn't catch on in England. People did not want to dig into Tibetan yak steaks, steamed Australian kangaroo, or Japanese sea slugs. But his society did bring ostrich, water buffalo, and bison farming to Britain.

Among the favorite dishes in Britain today: Toad in the Hole. Made (thankfully) with sausages, not toads.

Critter Matching

Each word on the left can be turned into an animal by adding a word from the box. We did the first to get you started.

1. BOB _____CAT_____
2. BUTTER _____
3. EARTH _____
4. GRASS _____
5. GROUND _____
6. JELLY _____
7. ARMY _____
8. PRAIRIE _____
9. SEA _____
10. STING _____
11. STINK _____
12. TAD _____

ANT
BUG
~~CAT~~
DOG
FISH
FLY
HOG
HOPPER
HORSE
POLE
RAY
WORM

Bonus: Combine two words from the BOX to make an animal. Can you combine two more words to make a second animal?

_____ and _____

Critter Making

Woof!

Combine pairs of words from the puzzle on the left page to invent new animals. For example, the one to the right is a POLEDOG.

Draw your critters here.

NOTE: You can use both the words in the box and the 12 numbered words (BOB, BUTTER, etc.).

Kowabunga!

When you hear the word boarding, *you probably think skateboarding or snowboarding. Well, here's a sport that's way . . . hotter!*

This Baby's a Blast

In volcanic terms, 2,389-foot-high volcano Cerro Negro (Black Hill) in Nicaragua is still a baby. It was born less than 200 years ago, on April 13, 1850. It started when a single volcanic vent erupted, blasting blobs of lava into the air. Lava blobs cool off in flight, so when they fell, a cone of dark volcanic rock and ash piled up around the vent. Result: a cone-shaped volcano made of cinders (ash).

Cerro Negro is the youngest cinder-cone volcano in Central America. Since its birth the cone has blown 23 times, with the latest eruption in 1999. You'd think that would keep people away, but it doesn't. Why? Cerro Negro is home to one of the world's newest extreme sports: ash boarding (or volcano boarding).

That's right. Volcano boarders don't zoom down snowy slopes. They slide down a steep cone of pulverized rock.

Are We There Yet?

There are no ski lifts for Cerro Negro. Boarders must make a sweaty 45-minute climb up the volcano's rocky backside. And they don't just have to get *themselves* to the top. They have to carry specially-made plywood volcano boards that weigh 15 pounds.

The view from the top includes gaping black craters on one side and a chain of hazy mountains on the other. The rotten-egg smell of sulfur fills the air and makes boarders think about the magma bubbling below the cone at temperatures of up to 2,192°F.

Biff, Bang, Boom?

For safety, boarders cover up with protective gear: special jumpsuits, kneepads, heavy gloves, and goggles. Most sit, but some stand, balancing on their plywood boards before shoving off. Pebbles and dust spew behind the boards as they swoop down the slope. The ride is bumpy, the noise deafening.

Boarding down a volcano at speeds of up to 50 miles per hour: a blast. Doing a face-plant on hot, rough, volcanic pebbles. a recipe for painful road rash. Some boarders make it down safely. But others wipe out, and even somersault down the hill.

So far, Cerro Negro is the only place in the world for volcano boarding. There are no professional volcano boarders and no competitions. But 10,000 boarders have plunged down the volcano's slopes to date.

Will the sport grow? Depends on the volcano. The biggest danger boarders face is not a wipeout. It's another eruption. Cerro Negro isn't just the youngest volcano in Nicaragua—it's the most active.

Order Yours Today!

Uncle John says, "Respect your elders!" Really. Even after you've seen these comic-book ads they fell for when they were your age.

The Toy: Bombs Away! Authentic bombardier cockpit
The Sales Pitch: "You'll feel like a real fighter pilot out on a bomber mission, blasting the enemy as our famous pilots did during the war. Comes with over 100 parts, including scale-model planes, ships, tanks, cars, and ammunition dumps. Realistic land and sea chart keeps you alert while dropping your bombs. Only $1.98."
The Catch: The cockpit was made of . . . cardboard.

The Toy: Grow 7 Monsters
The Sales Pitch: "Thrills and chills await you when you see seven amazing plant creatures come to life! Seven giant monsters in full, glowing color grow fantastic plant 'hair' before your eyes! Order now and get extra-large supply of guaranteed live 'Monster Hair' seeds. All 7 monsters for only $1.00!"
The Catch: Ever seen a Chia pet? This was your grandparents' version.

The Toy: Cracker Jack Magnetic Car
The Sales Pitch: "Wear Mystery Control Ring and Drive Car Without Touching It! It's amazing. Drive this miniature Ford car by holding your hand over it. Goes

forward and backward at your command. Only 25¢ plus two Cracker Jack box labels."

The Catch: The miniature car was made of metal, and the "mystery control ring" was a magnet.

The Toy: Real Switchblade...Comb!

The Sales Pitch: "Nine inches long with pushbutton action. This is a REAL switchblade. The blade is a COMB!!!! Great for sideburns and mustaches, too. Only $4.00 + 50¢ postage/handling."

The Catch: Uhm . . . it was a comb.

The Toy: Vampire Bat

The Sales Pitch: "Terrorize your friends on those dark scary nights. Monster size. Authentic natural colors. Hideous 7 1/2" fangs. Eyes glow eerily in the dark. Rattles windows, climbs, crawls, jumps, floats in air—all at your command! So realistic it even fools other bats. Operates indoors or out, and only $1.00."

The Catch: It was a rubber bat dangling from a rubber band.

The Toy: A Real Texas Ranch

The Sales Pitch: "Own a mini ranch in Texas—one square inch! We'll send a legal deed and a map showing where your ranch is located. Send $2.00."

The Catch: All it takes to figure this one out is a ruler. (For more fun, measure your foot to see how many "Real Texas Ranches" you could step on at one time.)

Answers on
page 280

Eat This Crossword

Identify each food, then write the answer in the
proper spot on the next page, one letter per box.

Across

3 [2 words]
5
8
10 [plural]
11
14
15 [plural]

Down

1
2 [plural]
4 [plural]
5
6
7
9
12 [plural]
13

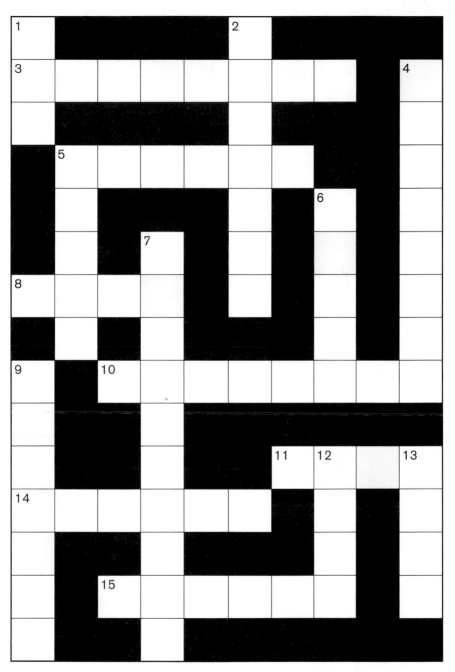

Bonus: Unscramble the letters in the yellow boxes to answer this riddle: **What has eyes but can't see?**

Cow Pies

Cow pies, cow flop, meadow muffins, cow chips and buffalo chips . . . there are lots of ways to say it. But by any other name it's still bovine dung.

The Inside Poop

A lot of cattle moved across the American West in the late 1800s. The big drives began in the spring so cattle could feed on new grass along the trail. And what goes in . . . must come out. Once the cow poop dried out in the sun, it turned into solid "chips." The fiber-filled chips made great fuel for cookfires. When wood was scarce along the trail, the chuck wagon cook burned cow chips. With one and a half million cattle on drives between 1865 and the mid-1870s, there was plenty of poop to feed the fire.

Dairy Doo

Cow pies are still used for fuel today. In Rockwood, Pennsylvania, 600 cows on a dairy farm produce 18,000 gallons of manure daily. Until a few years ago, that waste was pumped to a holding pond. "The odor was unbelievable," said the farm's owner, Shawn Saylor. Now the manure is used to create electricity— 1.2 million kilowatts per year. That's enough to power the dairy farm, and its neighbors, too. Bonus: The neighborhood doesn't smell like poo anymore.

Better Bricks

In Indonesia, a group of business students created a new type of brick called "EcoFaeBrick." The high quality, low-priced bricks are 20% lighter and 20% stronger than traditional clay bricks. The main ingredient: cattle dung. (And, no, they don't stink.)

B-i-n-g-oops!

It's been called "bossy bingo," "bovine bingo," and "cow pat lottery." But in Wells, Minnesota, it's known as Cow Plop Bingo. Once a year, a grassy field in a city park is divided into a painted grid of 300 squares. Rights to a square cost $5. Two cows are hauled in from a neighboring farm, and people wait for them to do their business. If a cow poops on a ticket holder's square, that lucky person can win up to $250. But cows sometimes take their time. One year contest officials had to draw a winner's name out of a hat. Why? The cows "held it" for three hours.

Live and Let Fly

Imagine throwing a Frisbee made of dried cow dung. Believe it or not, cow-chip throwing has been a popular sport since 1970. Beaver, Oklahoma, bills itself as "The Cow-Chip-Throwing Capital of the World." The rules are simple. The chips must be at least 6" in diameter, everyone gets two throws, and no gloves are allowed.

The longest cow-chip throw on record is 182 feet, 3 inches. It was set in 1979 by 22-year-old Leland Searcy. "I started playing baseball when I was seven," Searcy said. But the win wasn't just about his throwing arm. Searcy shared this chip-throwing tip: "When you go to pick your chip, you got to be sure it's a solid one."

• • • • •

Cow Quip Quiz

1. What do you get when you sit under a cow?

2. Why was the calf sent home from school?

3. What do you call a cow that can't give milk?

4. What's the best use of cowhide?

5. Why did the cow jump over the moon?

6. What do you get from a forgetful cow?

7. How do cows keep in touch?

8. What do you get if you cross a cow with a spaniel, a poodle, and a rooster?

9. What was the cow's favorite sci-fi film?

10. Which planet do cows like best?

Answers on page 280

Answers on page 280

Scrambled Eggs

· ·

Eggs can be laid by lots of different animals.
Unscramble each set of letters to reveal a dozen egg layers.

Birds:
1. BROIN
2. OSEGO
3. HEKNCIC
4. SCHOIRT
5. GALEE
6. CDKU

1. __ __ __ __ __
2. __ __ __ __ __
3. __ __ __ __ __ __ __
4. __ __ __ __ __ __ __
5. __ __ __ __ __
6. __ __ __ __

Others:
7. GORF
8. KENSA
9. TREULT
10. OSADRUIN
11. DRESIP
12. SIFH

7. __ __ __ __
8. __ __ __ __ __
9. __ __ __ __ __ __
10. __ __ __ __ __ __ __ __
11. __ __ __ __ __ __
12. __ __ __ __

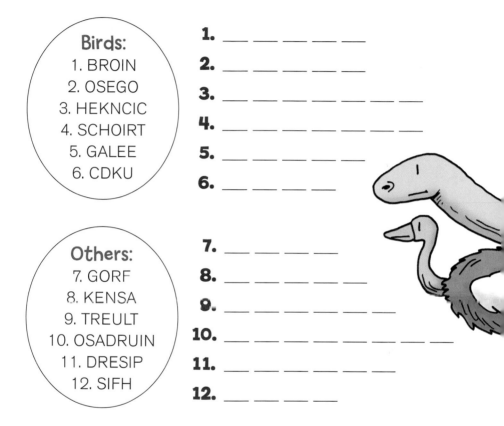

Unscramble these words that can come before or after EGG.

13. DIFER : __ __ __ __ __ ◯

14. RESTEA: __ __ __ __ __ __ __ ◯

15. ◯ __ __ __ __ __ __ : SLELH

16. ◯ __ __ __ __ __ __ __ :TRABEE

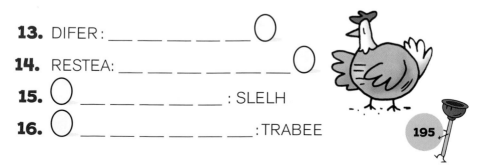

195

Beady-eyed

Find your way through this twisting
necklace of beads and beady-eyed charms.

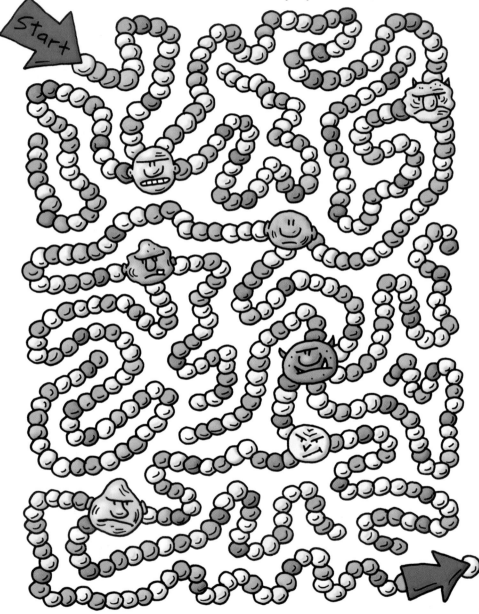

Start

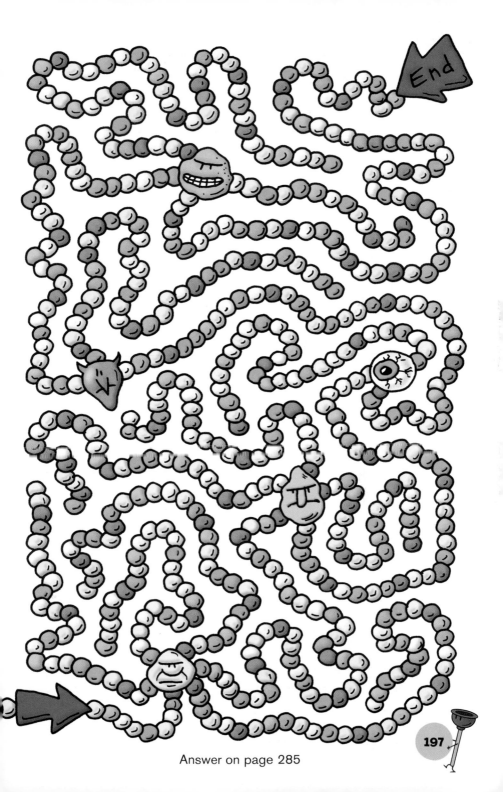

End

197

Answer on page 285

Dino Chompers

Bite into these juicy facts about dinosaur teeth.

The Lawnmower

Named for the Republic of Niger, the country where it was found, *Nigersaurus* (NYE-jer-SORE-us) also has a nickname—"the lawnmower." The 45-foot-long plant-eater had more than 1,000 teeth in its wide shovel-like mouth. It could mow down—and gobble up—a lot of lawn.

But when the thousand-toothed herbivore met *Sarcosuchus* (SAR-koh-SOO-kiss), its mighty crocodilian foe, that mouthful of teeth didn't help. Chicago paleontologist Paul Sereno says that *Sarcosuchus* would have feasted on the sauropod—toothy or not. "A lightly-built plant-eater would have been easy prey," he says.

The Fanged

About 125 million years ago, a feathered raptor the size of a turkey roamed the forests of what is now northern China. *Sinornithosaurus* (sye-NOR-ni-thuh-SORE-us)—the "Chinese bird-lizard"—was small for a dinosaur. But this bird ancestor had teeth. Two of them were very long and sharp. They curved backward in the raptor's upper jaw. Enpu Gong of the Chinese Academy of Sciences says they were so long they looked like saber teeth or fangs.

Deep grooves ran down the outer edge of each

sharp tooth. Rear teeth with grooves like these are found in only one kind of animal: the venomous kind.

Despite those nasty fangs, *Sinornithosaurus* had delicate jaws. It could not have handled a "grab and gulp" attack, injecting venom into its victim like a rattlesnake. Kansas paleontologist David Burnham thinks it might have been a "grab and hold" predator, like a python.

As *Sinornithosaurus* held the prey in its mouth, poison may have trickled down the grooves to disable the animal. Then it could have chewed the venom from its fangs into the open wounds . . . and waited for its meal to stop moving.

The Cannibal

The short-snouted *Majungasaurus* (mah-JUNG-ah-SORE-us) lived in Madagascar, an island off the coast of Africa, about 70 million years ago. The 23-foot-long dinosaur had dagger-like teeth and a taste for the flesh of its own kind. At least, that's what paleontologist Ray Rogers thinks.

At the time, the world was changing. Lakes and rivers dried up. Plant-eating dinosaurs became scarce. So meat-eaters had to look elsewhere for food. Rogers found the fossilized bones of a young *Majungasaurus*. The bones had tooth marks on them that matched the size and spacing of an adult *Majungasaurus*'s teeth. The bones had been gnawed and gnawed to get every scrap of meat.

"If you gotta eat, you gotta eat," Rogers said.

Sci-Fi Predictions

Although these books were written long before highways, space travel, and computers, their authors saw the future.

Gulliver's Travels (1726)

Background: English author Jonathan Swift lived more than a century before electricity was available. His novel follows a man named Gulliver as he encounters strange things in strange lands.

Prediction: *The computer.* In the story, Gulliver finds a "giant Engine" full of "Bits" of information that allow even "the most ignorant Person to write Books." Like today's electronic devices, Verne's engine was "linked together by slender Wires."

From the Earth to the Moon (1865)

Background: French author Jules Verne wrote this novel about a manned mission to the Moon more than 100 years before NASA landed astronauts Neil Armstrong and Buzz Aldrin there in 1969.

Prediction: *Manned moon missions.* The first real mission to the moon—Apollo 11—and Verne's fictional mission share strange similarities. Verne's moon trip was launched from Florida; so was the Apollo spaceship. Verne's ship carried three men and splashed back down to Earth in the Pacific Ocean. So did the real mission. (One thing that Verne got wrong: His spaceship was launched from a cannon!)

"The Brick Moon" (1869)

Background: This short story was written by American author Edward Everett Hale.

Prediction: *The International Space Station.* In the story, several countries share the high cost of launching a ship into orbit that people will live on for long periods. In the 1990s, that prediction came true.

Anticipations (1901)

Background: In H.G. Wells's time, people either traveled by foot or by horse-drawn carriage. For long trips, they took ships and trains, which were powered by steam. The car was a brand-new invention. And most people disliked it. Cars were slow, noisy, and they broke down a lot.

Prediction: *The 20th century would be dominated by cars.* Wells wrote that oil-powered engines would replace steam engines. Roads, most of which were dirt in 1901, would become wider, requiring speed limits to keep drivers safe. He predicted that people would move out of cities—where most lived in his time—into suburbs (which didn't even exist yet). He even correctly predicted that the region between Boston, Massachusetts, and Washington, D.C., would become one long system of cities, suburbs, highways, and ... traffic jams.

Which snakes are found on cars?

Windshield vipers.

Answers on
page 280

Bird Doodles

Which caption goes with which doodle?

1. ___

2. ___

3. ___

4. ___

5. ___

6. ___

A. bald man hit by bird poop
B. two birds in a
three-legged race
C. bird doing a beakstand

D. bird that fell in a
gopher hole
E. bird with fake teeth
F. a spring chicken

Your Bird Doodles

Create your own doodles, with a description below each one.

Really Big Food

Even Uncle John couldn't finish off
one of these monster meals.

Yo-Ho, Yum!

In 2002, Jacques and Antoine Tokar began sculpting a model of an 18th-century pirate ship. They had to work in freezing conditions. Why? They carved the ship out of 450 gallons of chocolate and vanilla ice cream. The ship weighed 2,039 pounds and set a Guinness World Record.

Burgerzilla

Until 2010, the record for the biggest burger ever made was 186 pounds. In 2010, eleven Canadian cooks beat the record with a 590-pound burger. But in 2011, the U.S. took back the title with a massive 777-pound burger. A crew of 10 cooks at the Alameda County Fair in California spent 13 hours grilling the burger. When the burger was done, it took a forklift to hoist it onto a 110-pound bun. Next they slathered on ketchup and mayo. Then they topped the burger with 13 pounds of lettuce, 20 pounds of onions, and 12 pounds of pickles. How big is a 777-pound burger? More than 1,000 times bigger than your dinner plate.

Are We There Yet?

If you hopped in the family car, started driving at one end of the world's longest sausage and drove to the other end, it would take half an hour to get there. That's because the sausage is 36 miles long! It was made in 2000 by chefs at the United Kingdom's largest sausage-making company, J.J. Tranfield.

Fork(lift) It Over

Got a sweet tooth? Then you'd have loved the world's biggest wedding cake. It was baked in 2004 by pastry chef Lynn Mansel and a team of more than 50 helpers. The cake's layers were so big and so heavy that workers had to use forklifts to stack them.

When the cake was done, it had seven layers and stood 17 feet tall. It weighed as much as a full-grown elephant: 15,032 pounds. And it was big enough to feed 60,000 people.

Home for the Holidays

In 2006, Roger A. Pelcher built a holiday gingerbread house for the Mall of America that would have made Hansel and Gretel drool. The cookie palace was 35 feet wide, 45 feet long, and 60 feet high. Best of all: The whole house was edible. The gingerbread-house builders used icing to cement the cookies together. And they decorated their palace with more than 2,000 pounds of chocolate bars, licorice sticks, and gumdrops.

Answers on
page 280

Your Fortune

No Chinese cookie or daily horoscope needed!
Using the column of your birth month, write down the
letters in the order shown to get some important advice.

Write the letters here, then break them into words:

___ ___ ___ ___ ___ ___ ___ ___ ___ ___ ___ ___ ___ ___
3   1   12 7   4   14 2   8   11 5   13 6   10 9

	JAN	FEB	MAR	APR	MAY	JUN	JUL	AUG	SEP	OCT	NOV	DEC	
1	V	A	O	M	A	I	E	R	O	A	T	C	1
2	L	E	U	E	K	M	O	N	A	O	B	E	2
3	A	S	H	I	T	S	W	C	D	C	S	A	3
4	D	T	R	A	L	N	A	L	T	P	I	I	4
5	H	R	T	O	W	H	O	R	E	E	T	O	5
6	N	O	D	B	T	O	H	L	E	A	D	K	6
7	I	U	A	T	K	O	R	W	O	L	Y	L	7
8	E	V	N	A	E	U	W	C	T	P	E	A	8
9	S	E	Y	T	H	M	T	S	Y	K	Y	Y	9
10	T	N	A	A	C	O	A	E	R	C	A	E	10
11	P	E	D	W	A	S	B	I	C	L	D	M	11
12	O	L	P	I	L	T	A	A	N	L	A	T	12
13	A	Y	O	M	I	R	Y	C	L	M	O	N	13
14	E	E	O	T	I	A	C	I	E	E	N	K	14

Alliteration Week

Alliterative words share similar sounds. Here are some fun facts about alliterative weekdays.

"Manic Monday": This is a 1986 hit song by the pop band, The Bangles. It's about a woman who wakes up on Monday and wishes it was still the weekend.

Two-for-Tuesday: Not a lot happens on Tuesdays, so many FM radio stations like to liven it up by playing two songs in a row from every artist. Double the fun!

Wacky Wednesday: Dr. Seuss's 1974 book is about some very weird things in the middle of the week—like shoes on the ceiling and a plane in the street!

Thankful Thursday is a movement that reminds people they don't just need to be thankful on Thanksgiving. Every Thursday is a time to stop and remind yourself what you're thankful for.

Freaky Friday: In this 1972 book by Mary Rodgers, young Annabel wakes up on Friday to discover that she and her mother have switched bodies. The horror!

Silly Saturday is our favorite day to goof off and come up with silly word articles. Like this one.

Super Sunday is the Super Bowl! For many, it's a big football game. (For us, it's a chance to eat pizza.)

Answer on page 285

The Drawer Goblins

Want to know exactly how bad a goblin's fashion sense can be? Then pay close attention to the clues in this Bathroom Reader Minute Mystery.

It bites living in a haunted house. Every morning I have to deal with something most folks never dream of—drawer goblins. They don't jump out and scream "boo" or drip slime on my feet. No. It's much worse. They won't let me choose my own outfits.

Today, after a deep breath, I pulled open the dresser. "Morning!" Horace stretched. He's the goblin that's lived here the longest—going on three years now.

"We have the best outfit for you today!" chirped Babcock. He's the new guy. About six months ago he moved in and started slobbering on everything.

I groaned. "Please say my shirt won't be covered with drool like it was yesterday."

Babcock cackled. "Drool dries," he said.

Horace held out my first item of clothing.

"Are you kidding?" I said. "Aunt Carly sent those to me from Bermuda. They're the color of Pepto-Bismol! I can't wear those. I'd never live it down."

"Just try them," said Babcock.

I used to refuse to wear anything the drawer goblins picked out. Then they got revenge. They turned all of my underwear ectoplasm green.

So I pulled on the hideous shorts.

Babcock offered me a second article of clothing,

something my grandpa had bought me for Christmas.

"No!" I begged. "Please. I'll look like I'm eighty."

The goblins cracked up.

"That's the idea," said Horace.

"Besides, your ancestors are Scottish, right?"

I glared at Babcock. "Not all Scots wear—"

"Wait!" Horace interrupted, scratching the wart on his nose with a grimy fingernail. "I'm sure we can find a bagpipe in here to complete the ensemble."

"No!" I grabbed the shirt and slammed the drawer before he could make good on his threat. Then I stuffed my feet into my favorite sneakers and ran to catch the bus.

In homeroom, I scrunched down in my seat, hoping no one would notice today's goblin-chosen outfit. It didn't work. Malcom Hockney walked by and sniggered. After three years of lame comments, I'd had it. "You got somethin' to say?" I asked. "Go ahead. Spit it out."

Malcolm looked at my shirt. He looked at my shorts. Then he looked at my feet, rolled his eyes, and nodded. "Yeah," he said. "Nice sneakers."

I glanced at my Quacky Duck high-tops and burst out laughing. "Thanks," I said. "I picked them out myself."

Can you guess what the boy in the story is wearing?

Answer on page 280

The Ig Nobel Prize

Who says science is boring?

Nobel? Not!

You may have heard of Nobel prizes. They're very serious awards for very serious research. But since 1991, a group called Improbable Research has awarded prizes to scientists whose work is . . . a bit odd. Or, as the award presenters explain, research "that first makes you laugh, and then makes you think." Here are some of our favorites.

2000 Physics Prize

Scientists in The Netherlands figured out how to make a frog float . . . in the air. They put the frog inside a strong magnetic field. The atoms in the frog's body acted like billions of tiny magnets that pushed against the field and lifted the frog into the air.

2001 Biology Prize

A Colorado inventor created underwear that removes the bad smell from farts before they can escape.

2003 Economics Prize

The nation of Liechtenstein found a new way to make money. How? The government rents out the whole country for parties, bar mitzvahs, and other gatherings. The cost: $70,000 a night.

2004 Public Health Prize

An Illinois high-school student disproved the "Five Second Rule." The rule says that food is safe to eat if it stays on the floor for less than 5 seconds. Not true! The student dropped gummy bears onto tiles covered with *E. coli* bacteria. The bacteria jumped from the tiles to the gummy bears in less than 5 seconds.

2005 Economics Prize

A Massachusetts professor invented an alarm clock that runs away and hides. You have to get out of bed to find it before you can turn off the alarm. The clock is supposed to help you get to work (or school) on time.

2007 Medicine Prize

Doctors conducted studies to find out if sword swallowing can cause sore throats, chest pains, or stomach bleeding. The findings: Yes, yes it can. And if sword swallowers get distracted? Double ouch!

2008 Biology Prize

French biologists found that fleas that live on dogs can jump higher than fleas that live on cats.

2010 Engineering Prize

Scientists from England and Mexico worked together to create a way to collect whale snot. They used a remote-control helicopter.

Pseudonymania

*Like Superman, some writers use fake names
(pseudonyms). Here are two poems by . . .?
If you discover their real names, let us know!*

The Twelve Months
by Sir Gregory Gander
(*not his real name*)

Snowy, Flowy, Blowy,

Showery, Flowery, Bowery,

Hoppy, Croppy, Droppy,

Breezy, Sneezy, Freezy.

Ele-Oops!
by Madame Tailfeather
(*not her real name, either*)

An elephant with floppy ears

Isn't wellaphant, I fear.

His cheeks are flushed. His trunk is red.

He really should go back to bed.

If from his trunk a sneeze should blow

He'll lose his elepants, you know.

Ah...
ah...

Pseudo Whodo?

All but two of these pseudonyms were used by real authors. And one of them is a member of the Bathroom Readers' Institute. Guess who's who!

Fake Name	Real Name
Sir Frizzle Pumpkin	Rev. James White
Smelfungus	Patrick Alexander
N.D. Toilet	Roscoe Duck
Lemony Snicket	Daniel Handler
Alexander the Corrector	Alexander Cruden
Dr. Slop	Sir John Stoddart
Lord No Zoo	John Swinton
Rock Cod	Phineas Phish
Dudu	Julia Fletcher
Sue Denim	Dav Pilkey
Ol' Jaybeard	Jay Newman
Hugo Playfair	Paul Paterson
Silence Dogood	Benjamin Franklin
Found Dead	James Payn
Dodenius Duckworth	Dr. Asa Greene

Answers on page 281

Odd Outhouses

Two of history's weirdest places . . . to go.

The Place: Acoma Pueblo

To Go: Talk about rooms with a view. Some very old outhouses sit atop a 350-foot-high sandstone mesa in New Mexico. They overlook a beautiful desert landscape. The mesa is home to the oldest inhabited city in the U.S.—Acoma Pueblo. Native peoples have lived in the pueblo since around A.D. 1075.

Why so many outhouses? Each of the pueblo's chiefs had to have his own. Once he was no longer chief, an outhouse would be built for the new leader. When asked about the outhouses, a local guide joked, "Those are our ATMs. They only take deposits."

The Place: Fourteen Foot Bank Lighthouse

To Go: Most of the lighthouses still standing today are on land. But this odd lighthouse sits in the middle of Delaware Bay. In 1886 workers sank a huge cast-iron cylinder deep into the bed of the bay. They filled the cylinder with rock and concrete to form a foundation. On top of the cylinder, they built a very fancy three-story lighthouse . . . with no bathroom. The outhouse juts over the edge of the cylinder, 20 feet above water. When the lighthouse keeper has to go, the poop plops right into the water. (Sorry, fishes!)

Creepy, Crawly Wall Critters

These critters are like sticky notes—put 'em on and peel 'em off as you please!

What You Need:

- Pen
- Con-Tact® Brand self-adhesive paper
- Scissors

Preparation:

1. Find a photo or drawing of the kind of bug you want to make. Trace the outline with a pen onto the back of the ConTact® paper, or just draw it freehand.

2. Use scissors to cut out the design. If you mess up, don't worry—limbs, wings, and other body parts can be re-attached.

3. Starting at its widest part, peel the bug design off the paper. Stick it to the wall wherever you want it to go, and stick on any spare body parts that didn't survive the cutting process.

Want to move your bug? Just peel it off the wall and re-stick it somewhere else!

I Saw a Sea Horse

Some big facts about a tiny ocean creature.

- *Hippocampus* is the Greek or scientific name for the sea horse. *Hippo* means "horse," and *campus* (or *kampos*) means "sea monster." But they're not very scary. The biggest sea horses are only about a foot long. And the smallest—pygmy sea horses—can be less than 16 millimeters long. That's smaller than a fingernail. (How scary can *that* be?)

- Pygmy sea horses were first discovered off the coast of Indonesia in warm Pacific waters. They live among coral reefs where water temperatures average about 84 degrees Fahrenheit.

- The weirdest thing about sea horses: "Dad" is the "Mom" . . . sort of. A pygmy mom lays five to eight tiny eggs into the "brood pouch" on Dad's belly. Dad fertilizes the eggs. Then blood vessels from his body provide nutrients to the eggs until they're ready to hatch.

- Once the eggs hatch, the father's belly contracts and burps the juveniles into the sea.

- Sea horse pairs mate for life. Once the male gives birth, he usually becomes pregnant again right away. Male sea horses spend almost all of their lives gestating their young.

- Most pygmy sea horses grow up just inches from where they left their father's pouch.

- Pygmy sea horses feed on plankton—tiny plants and animals that drift in the ocean but are too small to see. They suck in the plankton through their tubelike mouths and gulp it down whole.

- At night, pygmy sea horses like to stick together. They gather at coral reefs and hang out in groups of three to five.

- Pygmy sea horses have amazing camouflage. They hide *so well*, the first ones weren't discovered until the 1960s.

- One tiny sea horse has a pale pink body with red knobs on it and lives in pale pink coral that has red polyps on it. Its camouflage is so perfect, the first one discovered traveled all the way from its ocean home to an aquarium before it was spotted.

- Most pygmy sea horse species have been named after dive guides and underwater photographers. Why? They're the ones swimming around coral reefs looking for them.

- *Hippocampus denise* is often called the "plucked chicken pygmy sea horse." It is light yellow in color and doesn't have the typical bumps (called *tubercles*) most pygmy sea horses have.

- One pygmy species, named after dive guide Satomi Onishi, may be the smallest sea horse of all. Two Satomi's pygmy sea horses would fit across the face of a penny—with their tails stretched out.

Sea Horse Seekers

Where would you hide if you were only half an inch long? This game will help you find out, even if your shrink-ray is in the shop.

Object of the Game: Be the first to find a hidden pygmy sea horse! (Read all about them on page 218.)

You'll Need: White paper, scissors, and crayons

Preparation:

1. Give each player a half-inch square of paper to represent a pygmy sea horse.

2. Have each player search out a place to hide the sea horse square, without letting other players know its location. (Grandpa's nostrils won't do, unless he's willing to let you hide a pygmy sea horse in them.)

3. Pygmy sea horses exactly match the coral in which they live. They are almost impossible to spot. Have each player color the square to match the chosen hiding space. Take turns hiding sea horses while other players cover their eyes. (No peeking!)

How to Play: Yell "Go!" and then head out in search of the hidden sea horses. The first player to spot one collects the sea horse square and calls the other players back to base. Shout "Go!" again and continue in this manner until all of the sea horse squares have been found. The player with the most sea horses wins.

Toad Tongue Tanglers

· · · · · · · · · · · · · · · · · · · ·

One word has been removed from each of these
tongue twisters, which you need to put back in.

Once you've done that, try saying each one three times fast.

A. MARRIED	**D.** ANKLES	**G.** TOLD
B. PLUNGERS	**E.** BERT	**H.** ELEGANT
C. JEN'S	**F.** CHOKE	**I.** TIP-TOP

1. PLASTIC _____ UNPLUG FASTER.

2. JOHN JOINED _____ GYM.

3. MARLY _____ EARLY.

4. BIG _____ BURPED.

5. _____ ELEPHANT.

6. _____ KID-TOPIA.

7. UNCLE'S _____.

8. TOAD _____.

9. CROAK _____.

Did you know a group of toads is called a *knot*?

Great Job!

It's hard to believe, but some grown-ups actually get paid to do fun stuff.

Aircraft Repo Man

Thrills: Fly everything from 747s to helicopters to crop dusters. But first, you have to find the planes, no matter where they might be in the world.

Skills: These upscale "repo men" have to be as clever as spies to find the planes and as sneaky as thieves to repossess them. To get this job, you need a pilot's license, a passport, and nerves of steel.

Who Foots the Bill: Planes cost millions, and if a buyer doesn't pay up, the bank that loaned the money for the purchase wants the goods back. Banks pay repo men a percentage of the aircraft's value, from $10,000 to $900,000 per recovery.

Shadow Shopper

Thrills: Buy everything from running shoes to cell phones. Go to movies, order take-out pizza, and chow down at the best restaurants. And you never have to spend a dime of your own money.

Skills: The ability to shop till you drop.

Who Foots the Bill: Stores, restaurants, movie theaters, and other businesses hire shadow shoppers to test how well their regular employees do their jobs. The pay? Up to $18 per hour, plus lots of free stuff.

Bike Tour Guide

Thrills: Pedal through scenic mountain ranges, dodge cars in bustling cities, or cruise along some of the most beautiful coastlines in the world.

Skills: Bike guides must be skilled cyclists and in good physical shape. To lead tours, guides need to know about the history and culture of the area where they're cycling. If you want this job, you need to speak the local language . . . or learn it fast!

Who Foots the Bill: Travel and tour companies pay bike tour guides $75 to $150 per day, plus room and board, and expenses. A good guide also gets tips from grateful tourists

Movie Extra

Thrills: Eat a burrito, scream in a sports stadium, dodge (fake) bullets, fall into an icy lake in the dead of winter . . . there's no limit to what extras do.

Skills: Must be able to follow directions and not gawk at the movie stars (when the cameras are rolling).

Who Foots the Bill: Film companies pay extras $7 per hour or up to $150 per day. As an added perk, some extras work their way into speaking roles. Just ask Brad Pitt or Megan Fox, both of whom started their careers as extras.

Woof! Meow!

Each dog or cat has a name that matches what it looks
like or what it's doing. Can you figure out who's who?
For example, a dog with a fishing pole would be named Rod.

1. ART **2.** CAROL **3.** CLIFF **4.** DAISY **5.** SPIKE
6. PEARL **7.** RICH **8.** ROCKY **9.** SANDY **10.** JOY

A. ____

B. ____

C. ____

D. ____

E. ____

Fa
la
la
la

Xmas
Songs

DO-IT-YOURSELF:
Try drawing a dog or
cat with a name that
fits. Dot? Fanny? Jack?
Lance? Lincoln? Peg?
Use a separate piece
of paper if you need
more room.

F. ____

G. ____

H. ____

Yippee!

I. ____

J. ____

Kid-eating Eagles

For centuries, New Zealanders have told tales of giant birds that swooped down to carry away human children. Here's what scientists say.

A Bird-Eat-Bird World

Until about 750 years ago, the most powerful creatures on the islands of New Zealand were . . . birds! In fact, few other creatures lived on the remote southwest Pacific islands. The bigger birds ate the smaller birds, with one major exception. The biggest eagle of all time—the Haast's eagle—preyed on an even bigger bird: the moa.

The moa was a lot like a huge ostrich or an emu. It only ate plants. It weighed up to 500 pounds, sixteen times more than the 30-pound Haast's eagle. But the moa had a problem: It couldn't fly. And the Haast's eagle could. The giant eagle had a nine-foot wingspan. And it could attack its prey at nearly 50 miles an hour.

The Legend Begins

There were no humans in New Zealand until about 750 years ago. That's when the Maori people paddled their canoes across the Pacific, from the islands of Polynesia to New Zealand's islands.

When they arrived, they found—so their legends say—a huge black-and-white raptor with a red crest and yellow-green wingtips. They called the giant bird *Te Pouakai* or *Te Hokioi*, words that sounded like the cry the bird made. And they swore that the fearsome bird could catch and kill a child.

Science vs. Story

Early scientists who examined the eagles' fossilized skulls thought it could not have killed humans. They thought its beak looked more like a vulture's. Vultures are scavengers. They eat only what they find dead. But modern technology shows something different about the eagle's tastes.

Two scientists, Paul Scofield and Ken Ashwell, used *tomography*—a type of computer scan—to take a closer look at the fossilized skulls. They compared the computer data to what is known about modern predator and scavenger birds. And they concluded that the Haast's eagle had the perfect equipment for killing prey.

When Eagles Attack

Scofield and Ashwell think the eagle probably perched high above its hunting grounds. It would sit and watch for prey. Then it would swoop down to deliver a fatal blow. Given its size, the Haast's eagle probably had talons as big as a tiger's claws. It would have used those knife-sharp talons to pierce the neck of its prey. And then it would have crushed its victim's skull.

That's exactly how Maori legends describe the attacks on humans. "Science supports Maori myth," said Scofield. "The Haast's eagle was certainly capable of swooping down and taking a child.

"It wasn't just the equivalent of a giant predatory bird. It was the equivalent of a lion." A *flying* lion.

No Mo-ah Moa

As it turned out, humans were even deadlier than the giant eagle. Because the only mammals in New Zealand seemed to be bats, the Maori ate a lot of birds. One of their favorite meals was the moa: the giant eagle's favorite food.

Within a few hundred years of landing on the islands, the Maori had hunted the moa to extinction. Without its main food source, the Haast's eagle soon followed. Both the moa and the giant eagle became extinct about 500 years ago. But the legend of the child-killing bird lived on. Thanks to modern science, we now know the story is . . . history.

Doubly Tricky

Here's a great magic trick that's easy to do!

1. Hand someone 10 pennies.

2. Have them pick a spot in the middle of a hardcover book you're holding (the kind with a removable cover).

3. Open to that spot and have them lay the 10 pennies in a row down the center.

4. Close the book and then tap it a few times saying, "I will now double your money."

5. Have them hold their hands as shown. Open the book to the pennies and pour them into their hands.

6. When they count the pennies, they'll find 10—plus one dime!

How It's Done: Before doing the trick, slip a dime between the book's cover and the book. It will slide out when you pour out the pennies.

Flapjacks from Space

Are aliens visiting planet Earth? If so, why? Here are a few of our favorite alien encounters and the wacky theories people came up with to explain the unexplainable.

August 21, 1955—Hopkinsville, Kentucky

The Story: One night, Billy Ray Taylor headed outside to the well to fetch a pail of water. About a quarter of a mile away, he saw a huge "shining object" swoop down and land. Sometime later, a 4-foot-tall creature with big, glowing, yellow eyes and large pointy ears showed up in the yard. Billy Ray took some pot shots at it with his .22 caliber rifle. The creature did a back flip and darted into the night. But then it returned. Again . . . and again . . . and again. It perched in a maple tree. It skittered across the farmhouse roof. It popped up in a doorway and peered through a window. Billy Ray managed to shoot some holes in the house, but bullets just bounced off the "alien" with a metallic *ping*.

The Theory: The creatures were fairies, not space aliens. Fairy expert Rosemary Ellen Guiley says the description sounds a lot like "beings described in fairy accounts." Fairies, she says, are "little beings with large magical eyes." They like to play tricks on humans. And, of course, fairies have pointy ears.

April 18, 1961—Eagle River, Wisconsin

The Story: Joe Simonton, a 61-year-old chicken farmer, was busy making breakfast when a glowing silver saucer landed in his driveway. Inside were three men with dark skin and hair. (Joe thought they looked like Italians.) They were cooking something that looked like pancakes on a flameless grill. And they gave Joe three of them. Joe gamely took a bite, but the alien breakfast "tasted like cardboard." Later, the U.S. Air Force ran tests on the "space pancakes." Results: They were buckwheat pancakes made with ingredients found on Earth.

The Theory: The pancake chefs were actually Detrimental Robots (DEROS). Sci-fi magazine publisher Raymond Palmer told the Air Force that the DEROS had hypnotized Joe Simonton. They "fed him the pancake story so that he would repeat it and appear truthful." Palmer believes that flying saucers come from the center of the Earth. Their evil purpose? "To spy on people and project tormenting thoughts into their minds." (And, apparently, to force them to eat totally tasteless pancakes.)

December 3, 1967—Ashland, Nebraska

The Story: At about 2:30 a.m., police officer Herb Schirmer was out on patrol. He spotted something on the highway—a shiny metallic craft with blinking red lights. When Schirmer got out of his car, green gas shot out of the craft, and he passed out. Later, under hypnosis, Schirmer remembered seeing gray lizard-like creatures. They had slanted black eyes, flat noses, and slits for mouths. They took him aboard their craft. "You will not speak wisely about this night," they told him. And then they let him go.

The Theory: The beings were lizard guys from the constellation Alpha Draconis. Former BBC reporter David Icke says lizard creatures want to control our world. In fact, he claims, the British Royal Family are all members of the "Reptilian Brotherhood." And they can shapeshift: Sometimes they look human, but at times they turn into 12-foot-tall lizard creatures. Icke claims that the secret entrance to the space lizards' underground lair is at Balmoral Castle in Scotland.

• • • • •

How to Spot a Space Alien

Think a space alien might be sitting beside you in class? Uncle John knows four ways to spot one.

1. Their job is to study Earthlings. In class, look for the person asking (rather than answering) questions.

2. They misuse everyday items. For example, they may use a credit card to scrape ice off a windshield.

3. They must stay in constant contact with their ships. The person always wearing earbuds may be using an alien communication device.

4. They don't understand Earth humor. So they often can't telling when someone is joking.

Alien Avocado

*Until little green men invade our planet, this is the
quickest way to come face-to-face with an alien.*

What You Need:

- Knife
- Small spoon

Ingredients:

- Avocado
- 1/2 teaspoon lemon juice
- 2 black olives
- Small, narrow wedge of cheese
- Cherry tomato

Preparation:

1. Cut the avocado in half. Put one half in a plastic
bag in the fridge to use later, and peel the other half.
Carefully remove the pit.

2. Rub the lemon juice all over the avocado to keep it
from turning brown.

3. With a small spoon, carve big eyeholes, tiny nostrils,
and a small mouth on the curved side of the avocado
half. Slice a narrow slit near the top of the head, and
cut a small corner off the cherry tomato.

4. Place a black olive in each eyehole.
Stick the narrow wedge of cheese
into the slit at the top of the head,
and set the cherry tomato piece
into the mouth hole. Snap a pic
to send to SETI (the Search for
Extraterrestrial Intelligence
guys), then eat your alien.
Before it eats you!

Going, Going . . . Gone?

The International Union for Conservation of Nature (IUCN) says these animals could soon vanish from the planet. Here's why.

Greater Bamboo Lemur

This small primate lives on the island of Madagascar off the coast of Africa. It has white tufts on its ears and round red eyes. And it can usually be found munching on bamboo. The problem: Farmers slash and burn bamboo to clear fields for planting. And bamboo makes up most of the Greater Bamboo Lemur's diet. As the bamboo disappears, so do the lemurs. Only 200 still survive.

Vancouver Island Marmot

These cat-sized ground squirrels have short, chunky legs, thick fur, small ears, and a bushy tail. But they are so rare, most people who live on Vancouver Island have never seen one. The species got stuck on the island about 10,000 years ago when an ice bridge that joined the island to Canada melted. Since then, the marmots have lived in burrows under the island's high mountain meadows. They hibernate for seven months a year. In fact, they only wake up to search for mates or give birth to pups. With fewer than 100 marmots on the island, it's gotten pretty tough to find a mate.

Be'er Sheva Fringe-fingered Lizard

Newly-hatched Be'er Sheva Fringe-fingered Lizards know how to protect themselves. When threatened, they flash their bright blue tails at natural enemies, such as falcons and egrets. The predators strike at the blue tail, the tail breaks off, and the young lizard escapes. Then a new tail grows in its place. After the third week of life, the little lizards know how to hide, so the blue fades away.

Escape from humans isn't so easy. As people build more and more communities in Israel's Judean desert—the lizard's home—this endangered lizard loses ground . . . literally. It needs space to burrow and lay eggs (three to seven per clutch). But up to 90 percent of its habitat has already been destroyed.

Andean Cat

This small South American leopard prowls at night, high in the Andes Mountains. It looks something like a tabby house cat with silver-gray or reddish-gray fur and a long, thick, ringed tail. The biggest danger for this shy cat is poachers; they hunt the cat for its fur. Goat herders are a danger, too. They kill the cat because they mistakenly believe it feeds on their livestock. In fact, the cat stalks the *vizcacha*, a rabbit-like rodent. Not a single Andean Cat lives in captivity, so the species cannot be protected. When the last Andean Cat is gone, the species will be gone forever.

Boo, Who?

More cool and creepy trivia about stars buried at the Hollywood Forever Cemetery. (See page 82.)

Peter Lorre (1904-1964) Lorre's creepy nasal voice sent shivers down movie-goers' spines for 35 years in films like *The Boogie Man Will Get You* (1942) and *The Beast with Five Fingers* (1946). And if you haven't seen those, you might still recognize his voice. It's the model for Ren's voice in the *Ren & Stimpy* cartoons.

Fay Wray (1907-2004) Wray screamed her way to fame in the classic 1933 film *King Kong*. She spent a whole day recording those screams. "I made myself believe that the nearest possible hope of rescue was at least a mile away," she said.

Darren McGavin (1922-2006) In the TV series *The Night Stalker*, McGavin played a reporter looking into some very strange deaths. On one show, victims were drained of blood by a vampire. In another, aliens sucked the bone marrow from zoo animals. (Eww!)

Mel Blanc (1908-1989) Bugs Bunny, Daffy Duck, Woody Woodpecker, and Porky Pig live forever on film. Mel Blanc—the man who gave them their familiar voices—kept the sense of humor that made him a legend till the end. The words on his gravestone echo Porky's famous final line: "That's all folks!"

Exquisite Corpses

Here at the Bathroom Readers' Institute, we love to play with words. Now you can, too!

Around 1925, a group of writers and artists called Surrealists started a word game. The first person started a sentence on a piece of paper. He gave it to the next person to add a word, and so on. Surrealists liked to put strange images in their work. So it's no surprise that they ended up with a "surreal" sentence: "The exquisite corpse will drink the new wine."

How to Play

1. Open this book to any page and write down the first noun you see. (Repeat step 1.)

2. Open the book to another page and write down the first adjective you see. (Repeat step 2.)

> **We interrupt this game for a boring (but useful) grammar review!**
>
> **Adjective**: a word that describes something (blue, grassy, fun)
>
> **Noun**: a person, place, or thing (George, desert, poop)
>
> **Verb**: an action word (sing, eat, grab)

3. Open the book to any page and write down the first verb you see.

4. You should end up with 2 adjectives, 2 nouns, and 1 verb. Use them to fill in this sentence: The <u>adjective</u> <u>noun</u> will <u>verb</u> the <u>adjective</u> <u>noun</u>.

Example: *The wrinkled lions will find the silly rock.*

Answers on
page 281

Bug Sudoku

These puzzles use four different bugs. Complete
each puzzle by drawing bugs in the blank squares.
There's only one way to do it following these rules:

Each row
must include ———→
all four bugs

Each large square
(with the bold lines)
must include all
four bugs ———————→

Each column
must include ←———
all four bugs

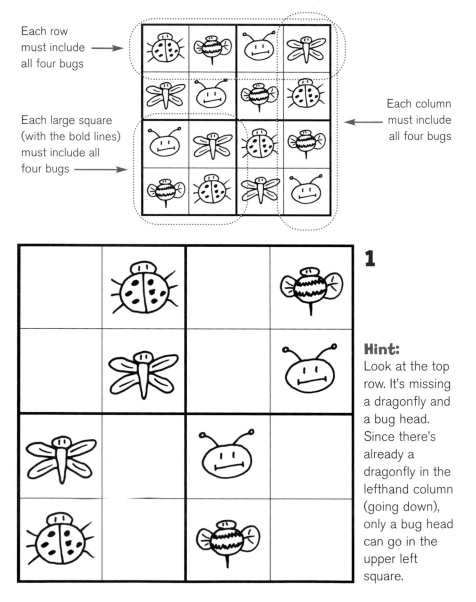

1

Hint:
Look at the top
row. It's missing
a dragonfly and
a bug head.
Since there's
already a
dragonfly in the
lefthand column
(going down),
only a bug head
can go in the
upper left
square.

2

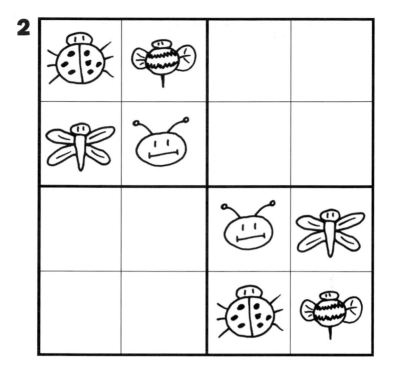

3

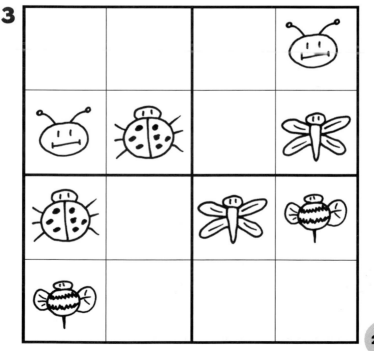

Dracorex hogwartsia

Meet the dinosaur Harry Potter would love.

Hot on the Trail

In the spring of 2003, three friends from Iowa—Brian Buckmeier, and Patrick and Steve Saulsbury—hiked into the rugged South Dakota wilderness. They slipped down deep ravines and climbed up steep cliffs. They scanned the ground, looking for anything that stood out, anything that might be odd. The hot sun baked down on their heads, but they didn't care. They were hunting for dinosaur bones.

Dig This!

Suddenly, Brian, who had gone ahead, came back around a bend running full out and yelling, "Skull! Skull! Skull!" Patrick and Steve raced with him to the site. "When we found the skull, all that was showing was a little of the snout and some teeth," said Steve. "But as we excavated more of it, it was clear we had something unique."

The friends took careful notes on the exact location of their find. And they mapped out the dig site, sketching and photographing the spot where they found the bones before they touched or disturbed it. They treated the site like a crime scene, knowing that sometimes there is evidence in how the bones are found. Once they'd mapped the site, they carefully removed all of the pieces of the skull from the ground. And they turned it over to the Children's Museum of Indianapolis for further study.

Scientists, including paleontologists Robert T. Bakker and Peter Larson, pieced together the skull bones to study them. And they agreed: This was a brand new kind of *pachycephalosaur* (pack-ih-SEF-ah-low-SORE), a two-legged, plant-eating dinosaur from the Cretaceous period (145 to 65 million years ago). With its flat skull, spiky horns, and long muzzle, the new dinosaur looked a lot like . . . a dragon.

Think My Name's Funny, Do You?

The new dinosaur was named *Dracorex hogwartsia* "The Dragon King of Hogwarts." (*Draco* means dragon, *rex* means king, and *hogwartsia* comes from the wizarding school created by author J.K. Rowling.)

According to the museum, Rowling was pleased. "The naming of *Dracorex hogwartsia*," she said, "is easily the most unexpected honor to have come my way since the publication of the Harry Potter books. I am absolutely thrilled to think that Hogwarts has made a small (claw?) mark upon the fascinating world of dinosaurs."

Brian Buckmeier was pleased, too. He sent Rowling a resin copy of the *Dracorex* skull, and she offered a gift of her own: an autographed Harry Potter book.

Joke-topia

Want a good laugh?
Start here.

Q: Do you know why the Mississippi is such a weird river?
A: Because it has four "i"s and still can't see.

Q: What do you call a cool rabbit that can rap?
A: A hip hopper.

Q: Why was the computer late for class?
A: He had a hard drive.

Q: Why don't skeletons fight each other?
A: They don't have the guts.

Q: What do you call cheese that's not yours?
A: Nacho cheese!

Q: What is more amazing than a talking dog?
A: A spelling bee.

Q: What do sea monsters eat?
A: Fish and ships.

Q: Why should you never tell an egg a funny joke?
A: It will crack up.

Q: What did the judge say when the skunk walked into the court-room?
A: "Odor in the court!"

Q: How do porcupines play leapfrog?
A: Very carefully.

Q: What did the hat say to the scarf?
A: "You hang around while I go on ahead."

Q: Where do bees go to the bathroom?
A: At the BP station.

Ice-Cream Fastball

*You don't need a machine to make ice cream,
but you do need a strong throwing arm!*

What You Need:

- Quart-size zip-top bag
- Gallon-size zip-top bag

Ingredients:

- 1 1/2 cups half-and-half
- 2 tablespoons sugar
- 1/2 teaspoon vanilla
- 24 ice cubes
- 1/3 cup salt

Preparation:

1. Put the half-and-half, sugar, and vanilla into the quart-size bag. Push out as much air as you can as you zip the seal. (Make sure it's completely sealed.)

2. Pour the ice cubes and salt into the gallon-size bag. Shake the bag once or twice, then put the quart-size bag inside and zip the bigger bag.

The Activity:

Grab a friend and practice your throwing by tossing the bag back and forth. After a few minutes, the mixture inside the small bag should turn into soft, rich ice cream that you can use to cool your aching arm before you sample it!

Scat's Amazing!

What's left behind . . . by animals' behinds.

Everybody Does It

All animals leave *scat*. That's what biologists call poop. They also call it *feces* (FEE-sees). Biologists can tell a lot about an animal by its scat: what it ate, how old it is, even if it's healthy or sick.

These days, your chances of seeing mammal scat are better than ever. Why? Because of "urban sprawl." More and more neighborhoods are being built where forests used to be. That means more wild mammals are wandering into neighborhoods looking for food. If you find some scat, you can figure out which animal left it there. Just like a biologist!

Warning! Scat can make you sick. Some animals carry diseases that can be spread through their poop. So just *look* at it. Don't touch it—ever. (Plus, it's gross.)

Here's the Scoop on Poop

● If the scat has fur, it was left by a *carnivore*. That's an animal that eats other animals. The fur belonged to its victim. Examples of wild carnivores that may live near you: foxes, coyotes, and mountain lions. They eat mice, rats, rabbits, and other small, furry animals. Sometimes you'll even find bird feathers in their scat.

● Examples of *domestic* (not wild) carnivores: dogs and cats. Why do we often see dog poop, but not cat poop? Because cats are very secretive. They bury their scat. If you find strange fur in your cat's litter-box, that means your pet ate a mouse or a rabbit.

• Deer leave behind piles of small pellets. If you look closely, you might see grass and other plant matter in the pellets. That's because deer are *herbivores*. They only eat plants. Other herbivores with grassy poop: cows, horses, goats, and any mammal with hooves.

• Two common nightly visitors: opossums and skunks. These mammals leave tube-shaped poops that look a bit like cat scat. And they never bury their feces. (So don't automatically blame the cat if you find suspicious poop in your garden!)

• Bears are *omnivores*. They eat animals *and* plants. Their piles resemble dog poop. But they're usually much bigger . . . and much smellier. If a bear-size pile smells sweet, look for berries in it.

• Raccoons eat lots of plants with seeds. And whole groups of them poop in the same place. So if you see a weird, poopy "garden" with a lot of weeds, that could be a raccoon bathroom. Some plants actually reproduce this way: Their seeds are spread by poop!

• Gross or not, lots of life goes on in scat piles. Flies, beetles, gnats, and other insects munch on the nutrients they find in animal feces. And some of them even call scat "home sweet home."

All the Presidents' . . . Shoes

Think you know all the important stuff about America's presidents? Bet you don't know this!

Why can't any other president fill Abe Lincoln's shoes? Because he's had the biggest feet (so far). He wore size 14 shoes, and his feet were just about a foot—12 inches—long.

Which president had "happy feet"? President William Howard Taft weighed 300 pounds and often got stuck in the White House bathtub. But that didn't keep him from dancing. Neither did not being able to tie his dancing shoes. His valet tied them for him.

Which president enjoyed a good spat? President Warren Harding. He liked to wear black shoes with brown button-down spats. Spats (short for *spatter-dashes*) go over the shoes and extend up the ankle.

Which president had the most "soul"? President Richard Nixon. He wore out his shoes so quickly he had to keep sending them back to be re-soled.

What did President Bill Clinton have in common with Elvis Presley? The 42nd president of the United States and the "King of Rock and Roll" both owned blue suede shoes.

Make Pepper Float

This experiment may seem like magic, but it's pure science.

What You Need:

- Salt and pepper
- Paper plate
- Balloon
- Your head

Preparation:

1. Shake some salt onto the paper plate. Shake pepper on top of the salt. Mix the salt and pepper together with your fingers.

2. Blow up the balloon. Rub it back and forth on your hair.

3. Slowly lower the balloon until it's about an inch above the salt/pepper mixture.

4. Don't freak out! The pepper will jump out of the salt and onto the balloon.

The Trick: The secret is static electricity. When you rubbed the balloon on your hair, you created a negative electrical charge. The salt and pepper have positive charges, and opposite charges attract each other. The salt and pepper were attracted to the balloon. But the pepper is much lighter, so it hopped onto the balloon and left the salt behind.

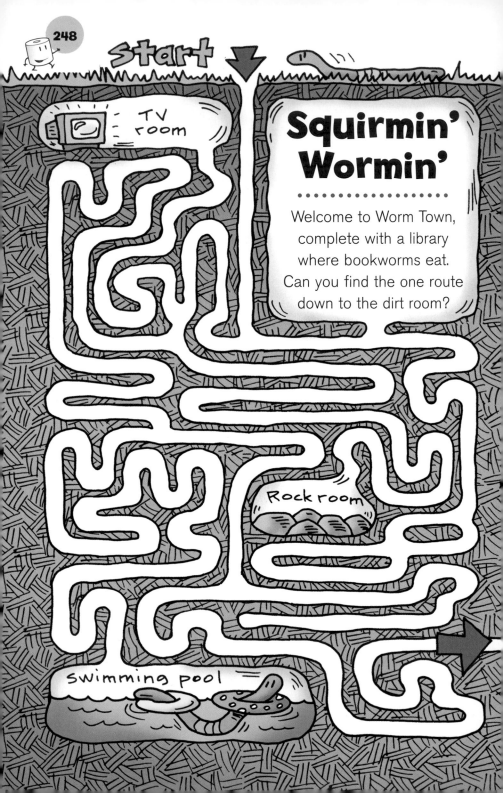

Answer on page 285

Giant Earth Fart

At least five times in the last 500 million years, most of Earth's creatures have disappeared in a geological blink of the eye. Why?

Oops!

About 201 million years ago, at the close of the Triassic period of Earth's history, something wiped out 70 percent of the life-forms on land and more than 90 percent of the sea creatures.

The massive die-off opened the door for dinosaur domination. But what caused this mass extinction event? Danish scientists at the University of Copenhagen think they know: a fart of truly epic proportions.

Feeling Gassy

First, a lot of volcanoes erupted. That released carbon dioxide (CO_2) into the atmopshere. Dr. Micha Ruhl, one of the scientists studying the mass extinction, says that the carbon dioxide "warmed up global temperatures."

As the temperatures rose, stores of another gas—methane—suddenly escaped. "Methane is only stable under certain temperatures," said Dr. Ruhl. "If it gets warm, it is released." That release was like a giant planetary fart. And it set off a deadly chain reaction.

Methane traps 23 times as much heat in the

atmosphere as carbon dioxide, the greenhouse gas many scientists blame for the current rise in Earth's temperature. So after the giant release of methane, atmospheric temperatures shot up.

Most plants died out. Without plenty of plants, *herbivores* (plant-eaters) couldn't survive. *Carnivores* (meat-eaters) couldn't live without plant-eaters to munch on. Mass-extinction events like this one open up the planet for new life-forms to take charge. In this case, dinosaurs survived when most other species did not. For the next 160 million years, give or take a few million, dinos ruled!

Oops, I Did It Again

Could methane trigger a similar Earth fart today? It's possible, Dr. Ruhl said, but it's hard to know for sure.

Today, methane is being released into Earth's atmosphere in many ways. Cow farts are full of it. One of the world's biggest beef producers, Argentina, has more than 55 million cows grazing its grasslands. Each of those cows produces about 66 gallons of farts . . . every day.

Methane is also released from landfills, coal mines, and leaking gas pipes. With Earth's temperatures on the rise, methane trapped at the bottom of the world's oceans is starting to escape again. "It's difficult to know how much methane is on the ocean floor these days," Ruhl said. "Maybe we have less methane on the seafloors. Maybe we have more."

Grab Your Gas Mask

Many scientists fear that Earth is already beginning to experience its sixth mass extinction. Some predict that by 2100, pollution, land clearing, and overfishing (plus those farting cows) may drive half of the world's ocean and land species to extinction.

Dr. Ruhl insists it's time for further study, not panic. "We have to remember that the world in the past was very different," he explained. "All the continents were still together; there were no glaciers. Ocean currents were probably very different."

But as Earth temperatures rise again, Dr. Ruhl says, "It will be interesting to see how animals and ecosystems cope." Including the mammals who now rule—human beings.

The Scoop on Poop

Plug your nose and take this quiz.

1. Which of these is not a word for outhouse?

a. Bog house
b. Necessary
c. The Drop Zone

2. Which of these three deadly diseases can be caused by water or food contaminated with poo?

a. *Escherichia coli*
b. Polio
c. Typhoid

3. The Roman god *Sterculius* was the

a. God of door handles
b. God of dung
c. God of ravioli

4. In the 1500s, how often did British parents change their babies' diapers?

a. Once every few days
b. Three times a day
c. When the baby pooped

5. How much did it cost to use the first public flush toilets?

a. A dime
b. A penny
c. Nothing

6. *Coleoptera scarabaeidae* is another name for:

a. The evil weevil
b. The dung beetle
c. The chicken-dung fly

7. Who was named the first head of New York City's Department of Street Cleaning?

a. George Waring
b. Thomas Crapper
c. Mr. Clean

8. Before toilet paper, people used

a. A sponge on a stick
b. Pages from books
c. Coconut husks

Answers on page 282

Maggoty No-Bake Brownies

Share these yummy brownies with friends, but save the "secret" ingredient as a surprise.

What You Need:

- Saucepan
- Food processor
- Bowl
- Spatula
- Baking pan or deep-dish plate
- Butter knife

Ingredients:

- 3/4 cup chocolate chips
- 1/3 cup evaporated milk
- 1 cup wafers or cookies
- 1/2 cup mini marshmallows
- 1/3 cup powdered sugar
- Pinch of salt

Preparation:

1. Use your fingers to press and twist each mini marshmallow into a long maggoty shape. Set the maggots aside.

2. Put the chocolate chips and evaporated milk in a saucepan. Cook the mixture over low heat until the chips melt.

3. Drop the cookies or wafers into a food processor, and pulse them until they are in very small crumbs. Mix the crumbs in a bowl with the powdered sugar and salt.

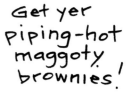

Get yer piping-hot maggoty brownies!

Yum!

4. Pour most of the chocolate mixture into the cookie mixture. Stir them together, and mix in most of the maggots.

5. Put the brownie batter into the baking dish or deep plate. Pour the rest of the chocolate sauce over the brownies, and stick the rest of the maggots in the top. Chill the brownies for at least 30 minutes before cutting them into squares.

Close Encounters of the Worst Kind

Remember Chicken Little? When an acorn hit her on the head, the silly chicken thought the sky was falling. Well . . . sometimes, it is!

What Fell: A meteorite
Who It Hit: 14-year-old Gerrit Blank of Essen, Germany
The Story: On his way to school one day in 2009, Gerrit saw a "ball of light streak through the sky." Then, he claimed, a red-hot space rock hit his hand, knocked him flying, and blasted a foot-wide crater in the road. The problem: Scientists say that even a pea-sized meteorite would blow a hole the size of a basketball in a person. Also, the chance of being struck by a meteorite and surviving is one in a million. Most sources think a bit of the meteorite bounced up and hit Gerrit *after* it plowed into the ground.

What Fell: A Delta II rocket
Who It Hit: Lottie Williams of Tulsa, Oklahoma
The Story: Lottie was walking laps in a park early one morning in 1997. She saw the sky "light up like the Fourth of July." About thirty minutes later, a DVD-size piece of metal mesh hit her shoulder. Officials believe it came from a spent Delta II rocket that had just reentered Earth's atmosphere. The U.S. Space Command tracks objects that orbit Earth and are

expected to reenter the atmosphere. "Every two or three days something falls back," said U.S. Space Commander Dave Knox. "Normally they burn up upon reentry." Lottie wasn't hurt. The blistered piece of mesh was as light as an aluminum can.

What Fell: A satellite
Who It Hit: 6-year-old Wu Jie of Shaanxi, China
The Story: In 2002, Wu Jie was playing with friends beneath a persimmon tree when thunder shook the sky and a 22-pound block of aluminum slammed into him. He ended up with a broken toe and a swollen forehead, but he was okay. The metal came from the outer shell of a satellite that had fallen from orbit and broken into pieces. Scientists predicted it would land in an uninhabited area. They were wrong.

Space Junk and You

Over the past 40 years, 12 million pounds of space junk has plummeted back to Earth. That's equal to the weight of 1,200 school buses falling from the sky. But don't worry: "The odds that one of the millions of pieces of trash orbiting Earth will fall and hit you are about one in a trillion," says Bill Ailor, director of the Center for Orbital and Reentry Debris Studies.

Why? Because 70 percent of Earth's surface is water, most space junk splashes into oceans. And if something does hit land, with an average of only 130 people per square mile, 99 percent of the planet has nobody on it at any given time.

Disgusting Defenses

These amazing, bizarre, and gross defense mechanisms help animals avoid becoming lunch.

Turkey Vultures can eat the nastiest, stinkiest dead animals without getting sick. While they're busy dining on the dead, it's easy for predators to sneak up behind them. If that happens, a turkey vulture will hack up undigested meat as an offering: *Here, eat this instead of me!*

The Spanish Ribbed Newt has two secret weapons: 1) a row of poison glands along the sides of its body; and 2) razor-sharp ribs. When grabbed, the newt flexes its body so that its ribs poke through those special glands and pierce through its skin, injecting poison into the predator. When the battle's over, the newt's wounds heal so it can fight another day.

The Hairy Frog (also called the Horror Frog) can sprout claws when threatened. How? It contracts its back leg muscles and breaks the small bones in the tips of its toes. The bones cut through the skin. *Voila!* The frog has claws like a cat on its back toes.

The Texas Horned Lizard spooks predators by squirting blood from the corners of its eyes. It can shoot up to one-third of its blood a distance of more than three feet. All of that spewing gore confuses the attacker and gives the lizard time to flee.

Fulmar Gulls got their name (which means "foul gull") because of the oily yellow vomit they yack up on other birds. At just four days old, fulmar chicks can puke on predators up to 18 inches away from the nest. The vomit turns the invading bird's feathers into a sticky mess so that it can't fly. Sometimes the invader falls right out of the sky.

The Hagfish. Want to know why the hagfish is sometimes called the "slime eel"? It's slimy! And with no eyes, no jaw, and no backbone, it looks more like an eel than a fish anyway. To defend itself, the hagfish oozes enough snot-like slime from its pores to fill a bucket. The slime either smothers the predator or gives the hagfish time to slip away. Once it's safe, the hagfish ties itself in a knot and squeezes itself clean by sliding the knot down its body.

That's Creepy!

- Frogs use their eyeballs to push food down their throat.

- A housefly's tastebuds are in its feet.

- The jaws of a snapping turtle can keep snapping for a day after the turtle's head has been cut off.

- Snails have teeth.

Picture This

TIP
It helps
to sketch
in pencil
first.

Here's an easy way to draw the picture on the other page. Just copy what you see in each square and—ta da!—a masterpiece!

Finish in ink, erase the pencil lines, and color.

Reel Stinkers

Just in time for your next movie night, here's our guide to some of the worst movies ever made.

Cutthroat Island (1995) Adventure

The Guide: A female pirate searches for a lost treasure and is rewarded with . . . a world record for biggest box-office flop (up until that time). Why? The movie cost $100 million to make and brought in $9.9 million. The director could have waged war on a small country with the battle-ready replicas of 17th-century ships he had built for the movie. Each one cost $1 million. But the film was so bad it sank.

Critics Said: "This film's motto: 'When in doubt, blow something up.'" —Kenneth Turan, *Los Angeles Times*

Son of the Mask (2005) Comedy/Fantasy

The Guide: Cartoonist Tim Avery's dog brings home the mask of Loki, the trickster god. Somehow, Avery's son is born with the mask's strange powers. He bounces off the walls, and—thanks to the movie's seriously creepy visual effects—his eyes (literally) pop out of his head.

Critics Said: "If you are the son of Frankenstein, Flubber, Dracula, Lassie, Ali Baba, Sinbad, Billy the Kid, Robin Hood, or Tarzan, you have to accept that the movie about you will not be as good as the one about your dad." —Jennie Punter, *Globe and Mail*

Spice World (1997) Musical Comedy

The Guide: British pop group Spice Girls get ready for a concert at London's Royal Albert Hall. Along the way, an evil newspaper owner tries to ruin their reputation. A friend has a baby. They hijack a (flying) bus—with a bomb on it. Police ticket them for flying a bus without a license and . . . frightening pigeons.

Critics Said: "This movie wasn't so much written as dripped. It's a fine waste of time for nine-year-olds."
—Cole Smithey, *The Smartest Film Critic*

Baby Geniuses 2 (2004) Comedy

The Guide: A group of talking toddlers use their superbrains to stop an evil media mogel from launching a satellite capable of worldwide mind control. The movie got a *zero* percent rating on the movie review site Rotten Tomatoes.

Critics Said: "A nappy load of crappy."
—Hannibal Wolff, *Yahoo.com*

Planet 51 (2009) Animated Comedy

The Guide: Astronaut "Chuck" Baker lands his ship on another planet. He thinks he's the first person to set foot on it until he steps on a green alien kid's rubber ducky. The movie lost 33 million dollars. *Squeak!*

Critics Said: "This was written by a bunch of monkeys trapped in a room with some typewriters."
—Anders Wotzke, *Cut Print Review*

Elephant Doodles

Which caption goes with which doodle?

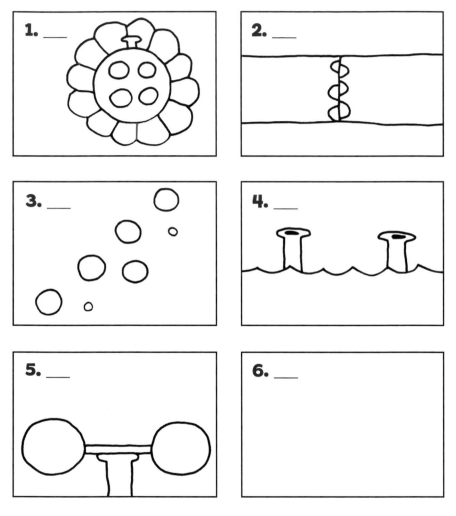

1. ___

2. ___

3. ___

4. ___

5. ___

6. ___

A. two elephants swimming
underwater

B. weightlifting elephant

C. white elephant in
a snowstorm

D. looking up at a
parachuting elephant

E. footprints of an elephant
with one peg leg

F. elephants shaking hands

?_____? Doodles

Write an animal above, then make your own doodles!

Animal Music

Think birds are the only creatures that can carry a tune? Think again. Here are some of our favorite musical animals.

The Elephant Orchestra: About 16 elephants at Thailand's National Elephant Institute have learned to play giant musical instruments. They play drums, harmonicas, and gongs. (They dance, too!) Many of the elephants used to work in the logging industry, dragging logs from the forest. But Thailand banned rainforest logging in 1989, putting the animals out of work. For those lucky enough to live at the Institute, playing music keeps them busy . . . and happy.

Mouse Music: When male mice sing, they sound a lot like baby birds. But don't bother putting your ear to a mousehole—most of the sounds they make are outside the range of human hearing. Scientists have recorded their music, and they used computer software to make the sounds loud enough to hear. The croonings count as songs because mice sing notes with different pitches—some higher and some lower. They don't just repeat a single sound over and over. And the phrases in their songs vary, like the lines in songs people sing.

Humpback Harmonies: Humpback whale songs can be heard underwater for at least 100 miles. Their musical sounds include humming, groaning, sighing, squeaking, and chirping. A humpback song usually lasts 8 to 15 minutes, and follows a definite structure with a repetition of sound patterns. Scientists think the songs are sung to attract mates, but they're not sure. Maybe whales just like to sing!

Frog Chorus: The Pacific chorus frog makes music along the west coast of North America, all the way from Mexico to British Columbia. They're small—only an inch or two long, but during mating season they get together and make a lot of noise. Male chorus frogs sing to attract females. During breeding season, huge numbers of males gather at ponds at night, and there's a whole lot of *krr-eek*-in' going on. You've probably heard them singing in the background of movies, because plenty of Pacific chorus frogs live in the Hollywood hills.

Tiny Strummer: A water bug called the boatman is the loudest animal on Earth relative to its body size. To attract a mate, the boatman uses stridulation, the act of rubbing two body parts together to produce a sound. Scientists used underwater microphones to record the bug's music. They discovered something amazing: The insect's songs reach up to 78.9 decibels. That's as loud as a passing train. But the bug making all that noise—it's no bigger than a grain of rice.

Answers on
page 282

Starts with B

• •

Every answer starts with the letter B.
Identify each picture and then write the word in
the proper spot on the next page, one letter per box.

Across

1

5

6

7

8

9

11

12

13

14

15

16

17
[plural]

Down

1

2

3

4

7

8
[extra
credit!]

9

10

14

Bonus: Unscramble the letters in the yellow boxes to answer this: **What do you call sea gulls that live on bays?**

The Body Bizarre

These facts about your body may be
hard to believe. But they're true!

- Your mouth makes enough saliva in your lifetime to fill not just one, but *two* swimming pools!

- Your nose can sniff out 50,000 different smells.

- No matter what color your eyes are now, when you were born they were blue.

- The strongest muscle in your body (for its size): your tongue.

- Good nose news: Your nose doesn't grow longer as you age. Bad nose news: Thanks to gravity, it droops.

- If you could hold your brain in your bare hands, it would feel like a three-pound block of tofu.

- Your body actually glows, but the light is 1,000 times too dim for your eyes to see.

- If you have red hair, you're more sensitive to pain than people with other hair colors.

- Exercise makes you smarter. Why? During exercise, the extra blood flow "feeds" your brain by bringing it more oxygen and nutrients.

- There are two kinds of earwax: wet and gooey, or dry and flaky. Wet earwax is useful for trapping insects that try to sneak into your ears. But if your ears have the wet kind, you have smellier armpits.

Zany Brainies

These kids are wicked smart . . . in a good way!

Enzo Monfre, Age 8, Science Show Host. One day, Enzo told his dad he wanted to create a TV show about science. "Great idea," his dad said. Enzo's dad filmed him talking about a praying mantis that he'd caught. Once the video hit YouTube, fans started emailing. Before he knew it, he was the host of his own show—*Enzoology.* Enzo's mission: "To destroy the idea that science is 'uncool.'"

Katie Stagliano, Age 10, Anti-Hunger Activist. The tiny cabbage seedling Katie brought home from school didn't seem like a big deal. And then . . . it grew into a 40-pound cabbage. Katie donated the giant cabbage to a soup kitchen, and it fed 275 people. Then Katie learned that 12 million kids in the U.S. go to bed hungry each night. So she designed a T-shirt to raise awareness. The front of the shirt reads, "My Dream . . . No Hungry Children." The back says, "It Will Only Take a Seedling."

Jonny Cohen, Age 11, Inventor. To keep him from taking apart everything in the house, Jonny's parents make a lot of trips to Radio Shack. In 2007, Jonny invented "Green Shields"—plexiglass panels that improve the gas mileage of school buses. His zaniest invention: a miniature camera sewn into a Beanie Baby to spy on his sister.

Maine's Mystery Monster

Ever seen something lurking in the bushes and thought it might be a horrible beast? This "beast" terrified people for fifteen years.

Roadkill

One day in the summer of 2006, a car struck and killed . . . something . . . on Route 4 in rural Maine. According to a witness, "It was charcoal gray, weighed between 40 and 50 pounds, and had a bushy tail, a short snout, short ears, and curled fangs hanging over its lips." Photos showed a creature with blue lips. The "whites" of its eyes looked blue, too. Some people claimed that when the beast was alive, its eyes glowed in the dark.

Was this the monster that had terrorized Androscoggin County for so long? For 15 years, residents of the area had heard "chilling, monstrous cries" at night. And something had killed at least two dogs and some livestock not long before.

Oo-Oo—That Smell

A woman had spotted the creature near her yard about a week before it died. "It was evil-looking," she said. "And it had a horrible stench I will never forget. We locked eyes for a few seconds, and then it took off. I've lived in Maine my whole life, and I've never seen anything like it." To her, it looked like a "hybrid mutant of something."

Backwoods Terror

People in Androscoggin County had been hearing and seeing a strange creature since at least 1991. Among the first was Martha David, who lived in a mobile home with her husband in the town of Litchfield. One cool autumn morning just before dawn, she heard something howl.

"There was a creature out there, and it was making a sound I can't describe as earthly," she said. "It sent a chill up my spine."

Leo Doyon, who had been hunting in the Maine woods for more than 50 years, first saw the creature in 2004. He thought he knew every type of animal that lived in Maine. But he'd never seen anything like this one. "It was no wolf," he said. "To tell you the truth, I don't know what it was."

An animal control officer had seen it, too. He thought it looked like a hyena. So what was it, really?

Night of the Cryptid

By the time experts arrived to look at the dead animal, there wasn't much left. Vultures had already eaten most of the carcass. But Loren Coleman, director of the International Cryptozoology Museum in Portland, Maine, did get a look at it.

Coleman is an expert on *cryptids*, mysterious creatures like the Loch Ness Monster and Bigfoot. This case reminded him of a rare black wolf that had been shot by a hunter in Maine back in 1993. The wolf had wandered down from Canada. Perhaps this animal had, too. But to Coleman, this animal looked more like a wild dog. And then he noticed something odd: The animal had extra claws. "They were sticking up like the horns of a devil," he said.

Scientific Testing

Hyena, black wolf, coyote, dog? No one knew for sure. Hyenas live in Africa, so that seemed unlikely. But wolves sometimes crossed into Maine, and coyotes were fairly common. Was this creature some kind of mix? Or was it a completely unknown animal?

A local newspaper sent the animal's paw to a lab for testing. DNA tests solved the mystery: The creature was . . . a dog. A second test said the same thing. Despite this proof, producers of the TV show *MonsterQuest* wanted to share the story. They asked Loren Coleman to help. "Why would you want to do a show on that?" he asked. "It's a dog." Case closed.

And ... Action!

You can make a mini movie using this book!

1. Turn the book sideways with the long side facing you.

2. Open to the last page and draw a simple stick figure in the lower left.

3. On the next to last page, draw the stick figure in the same spot, but with its head coming off slightly.

4. Position the head on each page so that it bounces across to the right as you go forward in the book.

5. Watch your movie by riffling the pages from back to front.

Or ...
A pad of self-adhesive notes works great, too.

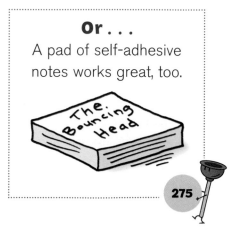

The Bouncing Head

The Answers

Maze answers start on page 283

Fowl Facts (page 14)

Numbers 2 and 5 are true.

1. There are close to 20 billion chickens on Earth, but each one would have to be about 200 feet tall to reach all the way to Saturn.

3. Wild chickens don't migrate and certainly not in V formations.

4. The color of an egg yolk can change a little depending on a hen's diet, but not the shell.

Say Uncle (page 19)

1. cone	6. close
2. neon	7. lunch
3. ouch	8. holes
4. echo	9. house
5. clue	10. ounce

Drop Down and Give Me Five (pages 22-23)

1. Cats cannot taste anything sweet.
2. A group of foxes is called a skulk.
3. A bald eagle nest can weigh one ton.
4. Beavers and rats are both rodents.
5. Hippos spend less time on land than they do in water.

Arm in Arm in Arm (page 33)

1. F   2. H   3. G   4. B
5. D   6. E   7. A   8. C

It's a Zoo in Here! (pages 54-55)

Bonus: PIG

Not-So-Super Superheroes (pages 58-59)

A. 9   B. 6   C. 2   D. 3   E. 7
F. 1   G. 5   H. 8   I. 10   J. 4

Brain Buzzers (page 65)

1. The turtle wins. After 10 yards, the turtle will be tied with the slug, 5 yards from the finish. We know the turtle runs two times as fast as the slug (he can run 10 yards to the slug's 5 yards). So when the turtle crosses the finish line, the slug will have covered only half of those last 5 yards, or 2 1/2 yards.

2. Because the amount of time is the same:
1 minute (60 seconds) +
20 seconds = 80 seconds.

3. 42. There are 21 eyes, but there are *two faces* on each card, so the total is double that. 8 eyes (queens) + 7 eyes (kings) + 6 eyes (jacks) x 2 = 42.

The Pirate Bride (page 67)

1. a buck an ear (a buccaneer)
2. gets wet
3. a squashbuckler
4. maroon
5. sir
6. on the poop deck

Shape Shifting (page 75)

Numbers 4, 6, and 8 can't be made from those two shapes.

Figure It Out (page 77)

Their favorite letter is T, because without it they'd be SICK FIGURES.

Mystery Joke (page 85)

Hold the bottom of the page just below your eyes and look up the page. That will shorten the letters so you can read the joke: WHY WAS THE SAND WET.

Read the same way from the right side to find this answer: BECAUSE THE SEA WEED.

Yay! Rats! (page 87)

1. brat
2. rating
3. crater
4. *The Karate Kid*
5. pirate
6. scratch
7. rattle
8. operator
9. marathon
10. Democrat
11. concentrate

Wacky Whazzits
(pages 96-97)

Number 6 is real, and you can make it. Cut a long, thin strip of paper. Twist one end of it so the opposite side faces up. Make a loop and tape the ends together. You now have what's called a "Möbius strip." Draw a line on it and you'll find it travels along both sides of the strip because . . . there's only one side! Fold the strip in three spots to make it more triangular, like the one on page 97.

Palindromania! (page 102)

1. drab
2. safe
3. pets
4. Loops
5. doom
6. nine men

Bonus: The three headlines in the story are palindromes from Weird Al's song "Bob":

   If I Had a Hi-Fi
   Never Odd or Even
   Too Hot to Hoot

Ship's Wheel of Fortune (page 113)

ONE DOZEN PIRATES

Turkey Talk (page 133)

These matches can go in any order:
A is the punch line for D.
G is the punch line for B.
E is the punchline for H.
C and F are not used.

What's What? (page 150)

| A. 8 | B. 5 | C. 7 | D. 4 |
| E. 3 | F. 6 | G. 1 | H. 2 |

Brain Farts (page 151)

1. Lincoln was sitting in a seat when he was shot. But he wasn't shot in his *seat*, which is another word for *butt*.

2. Using *bare* in place of *bear*. Bare means to expose. Bear means to carry. Wonder why the people would want to carry arms? In this case, *arms* aren't body parts; they're *weapons*.

3. Using *vermin* in place of *ermine*. Vermin are pesky insects or diseased animals. *Ermine* is a fur often used to trim royal garments.

4. Using *magnet* in place of *maggot*. A *magnet* is a piece of metal that attracts other metals. A *maggot* is a squirmy white insect larva that is attracted to rotten meat.

5. Using *tacks* in place of *tax*. The English put a *tax* (a fee to be paid to the British government) on tea. Even Mad King George wasn't crazy enough to put *tacks* (small sharp nails) in his tea.

6. Using *thorn* in place of *throne*. Ouch! We're hoping Queen Victoria sat on a *throne*, not a *thorn*.

7. Using *deacon* in place of *beaker*. A *deacon* is an officer or minister in a church. A *beaker* is a glass container used in laboratories. (The brain fart probably went like this: *beaker* became *beacon*,

which became *deacon*.)

8. Using *lion* in place of *line*. Sure, there are lions running through Africa. But, believe us, they're real. That imaginary thing running around Earth is a *line*.

9. *Pistols* in place of *pistils*. Cowboys carry pistols; flowers have *pistils*—the female part of a flower.

10. Using *taxis* in place of *taxes*. After the Revolutionary War the colonists did stop paying *taxes* to Britain. But not paying for taxis? Forget about it! (Especially in New York City.)

Ship Shape (page 156)

C. 1   I. 2   D. 3   A. 4   G. 5
J. 6   F. 7   B. 8   E. 9   H. 10

Crazy Crazes (page 157)

1. head
2. smell
3. trolls
4. caveman
5. pet
6. pizza
7. lamps
8. paper
9. pen

Tawkin' Bawstin
(page 160)

1. C   2. A   3. F   4. E   5. I
6. B   7. J   8. H   9. G   10. D

Moon Code (page 161)

rating: ONE STAR
food: OUT OF THIS WORLD
atmosphere: NONE

A Filling Joke
(pages 166-167)

ghost, bag, cookie, ladder, butterfly, stamp, bat, pillow, hat, brush, truck, spider, nest, fish, wave, camera
Joke answer: He was a light eater.

Critter Matching
(page 184)

1. bobcat
2. butterfly
3. earthworm
4. grasshopper
5. groundhog
6. jellyfish
7. army ant
8. prairie dog
9. sea horse
10. stingray
11. stinkbug
12. tadpole
Bonus: "Horsefly" and "catfish" are the most common ones, but there's also "dogfish", "hogfish", and "polecat" (a type of weasel or another name for a skunk).

Eat This Crossword
(pages 190-191)

Bonus: POTATO

Cow Quip Quiz (page 194)

1. a pat on the head
2. it moo-ned the teacher
3. a Milk Dud
4. to hold the cow together
5. because the farmer had cold hands
6. milk of amnesia
7. through instant moo-sages
8. a cockerpoodlemoo!
9. Steer Wars
10. Jupiter. It has the most moo-ns.

Scrambled Eggs
(page 195)

1. robin
2. goose
3. chicken
4. ostrich
5. eagle
6. duck
7. frog
8. snake
9. turtle
10. dinosaur
11. spider
12. fish
13. fried
14. Easter
15. shell
16. beater

Bird Doodles (page 202)

1. D 2. F 3. B 4. E 5. A 6. C

Your Fortune (page 206)

January: AVOID ELEPHANTS
February: SALUTE EVERYONE
March: HOP AROUND TODAY
April: IMITATE A WOMBAT
May: TALK LIKE A WITCH
June: SIT ON A MUSHROOM
July: WEAR A COWBOY HAT
August: CRAWL IN CIRCLES
September: DO NOT EAT CELERY
October: CALL PEOPLE "MACK"
November: STAY IN BED TODAY
December: ACT LIKE A MONKEY

The Drawer Goblins
(pages 210-211)

What is the boy from the story wearing? Pink shorts and a plaid shirt. Pepto-Bismol is bright pink, and Scots are known for wearing plaids and playing bagpipes.

Pseudo Whodo?
(page 215)

These two pseudonyms are fake: N.D. Toilet/Roscoe Duck and Rock Cod/Phineas Phish. And real Bathroom Readers' Institute writer Jay Newman sometimes uses the fake name "Ol' Jaybeard."

Three pseudonyms play with the difference between how the names are written and how they sound—N.D. Toilet (in the toilet), Sue Denim (pseudonym), and Lord No Zoo (Lord knows who). If you spotted them, you're a wordsmith in the making. Better start thinking up a pseudonym now!

Toad Tongue Tanglers
(page 221)

1. B   2. C   3. A   4. E   5. H
6. I   7. D   8. G   9. F

Woof! Meow!
(pages 224-225)

A. 6   B. 1   C. 5   D. 2   E. 7
F. 8   G. 4   H. 10   I. 9   J. 3

Bug Sudoku (pages 238-239)

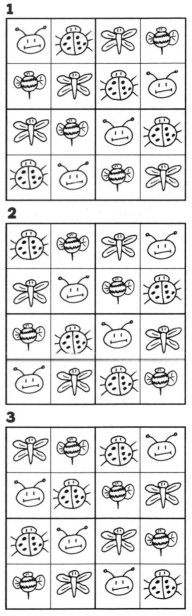

The Scoop on Poop
(page 253)

1. C. Both "bog house" and "necessary" are terms for an outdoor toilet in Britain.

2. All three answers are correct. These three diseases, plus others such as cholera and dysentery, can be caused by contamination from feces—that's another word for poo. Such diseases have killed more people than all the wars in the history of the world.

3. B. The weird thing is that the Romans really had a god for door handles, too: Cardea.

4. A. But at least they were a step up from the moss and leaves once used to clean babies' bottoms.

5. B. The first public flush toilets were at the Crystal Palace exhibition in London's Hyde Park in 1851. An inventor named George Jennings installed "halting stations" with flush toilets for park visitors, and 800,000 people paid a penny apiece to use them.

6. B. We made up the evil weevil, but the chicken-dung fly is a real insect. Guess where it hangs out?

7. A. Before Waring took over, 2.5 million pounds of manure ended up on New York City streets every day.

8. All three answers are (painfully) correct. Sponge on a stick (Ancient Rome); pages from books (British lords); coconut husks (Hawaii).

Elephant Doodles (264)

1. D 2. F 3. E 4. A 5. B 6. C

Starts with B
(pages 268-269)

bonus: BAGELS

The Mazes

Splat! (pages 28-29)

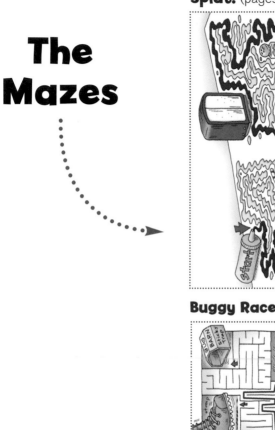

Buggy Race (pages 62-63)

Fairy Dusting (pages 80-81)

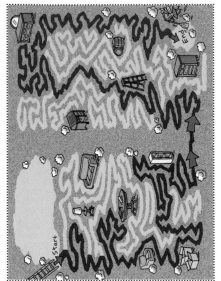

Which Liquid? (pages 106-107)

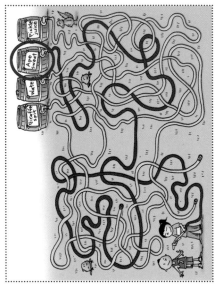

Down the Drain (pages 138-139)

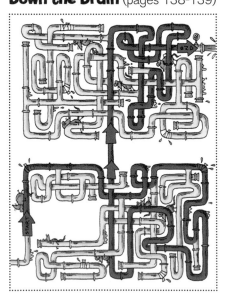

Ogre Drool (pages 154-155)

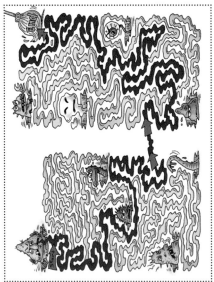

One Way (pages 174-175)

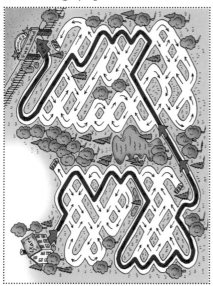

Beady-eyed (pages 196-197)

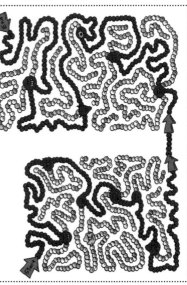

Diary Doodle (pages 208-209)

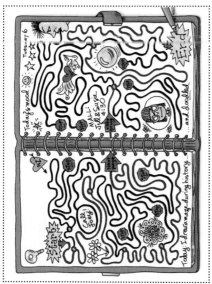

Squirmin' Wormin' (248-249)

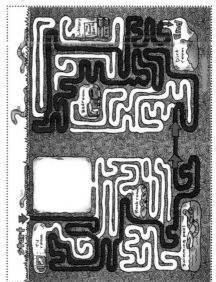

Come on . . .
TAKE THE PLUNGE!

To read a few sample chapters,
go to our website and visit
the "Throne Room" at

www.bathroomreader.com

**Also available
from the BRI—**

An ever-growing
assortment of
great gift ideas:

- **Calendars**
- **T-shirts**
- **Mini Books**
- **Puzzle Books**
- **E-Books**
- **Mobile Apps**
- **. . . and more!**

The Last Page

Fellow Bathroom Readers: Bathroom reading should never be taken loosely, so Sit Down and Be Counted! Join the Bathroom Readers' Institute. Just go to www.bathroomreader.com to sign up. It's free! Or send a self-addressed, stamped envelope and your email address to Bathroom Readers' Institute, P.O. Box 1117, Ashland, Oregon 97520. You'll receive a free membership card, our BRI newsletter (sent out via email), discounts when ordering directly through the BRI, and a permanent spot on the BRI honor roll!

UNCLE JOHN'S NEXT
BATHROOM READER FOR KIDS ONLY
IS ALREADY IN THE WORKS!

Is there a subject you'd like to read about in our next *Uncle John's Bathroom Reader* for kids? Go to CONTACT US at www.bathroomreader.com and let us know. We aim to please.

Well, we're out of space, and when you've got to go, you've got to go. Hope to hear from you soon. Meanwhile, remember . . .

GO WITH THE FLOW!